To Bonnie & Jim,
Love,
Dad

JUST DOGS

JUST DOGS

A LITERARY AND PHOTOGRAPHIC TRIBUTE
TO THE GREAT HUNTING BREEDS

WILLOW CREEK PRESS

CONTENTS

For True, Keyni, Sadie,
Wink, and Baxter

Published in the United States by
  Willow Creek Press
  PO Box 881
  Minocqua, WI 54548.

ISBN 1-57223-020-7
(Previously ISBN 0-932558-47-X)

First Edition: August 1988

Library of Congress
Cataloging-in-Publication Data

Just dogs.
      1. Hunting dogs—Anecdotes.
      2. Hunting dogs—Literary collections.
      3. Hunting dogs—Pictorial works.
      4. Hunting stories.
SF428.5.J87 1988
799.2'34   88-50861
              CIP

Printed in the United States of America.

PHOTOGRAPHIC CREDITS:
Erwin Bauer: page VIII. Daniel J. Cox: title page, pages 22, 28-29, 30, 79, 81, 88-89, 120-121, 124. Tom Davis: page 117. Chris Dorsey: page 69. George Bird Evans: pages 25, 100, 138. Greg Gersbach: pages 62-63, 108-109. Tom Huggler: page 48. Gerald C. Johnson: pages 47, 122. Peter Miller: pages X, 20, 54, 58, 59, 60, 92-93, 131. Dale Spartas: Cover, pages IV-V, 26, 32, 33, 34, 36-37, 50-51, 57, 65, 66, 67, 70, 71, 82, 83, 102, 104, 105, 106, 113, 114, 115, 119, 123, 126, 127, 133, 135, 137, 147. Gary Zahm: pages VI-VII, 12-13, 44, 85, 87, 91, 96.

ACKNOWLEDGEMENTS: The editors of Willow Creek Press would like to thank the following publishers and individuals for permission to reprint certain portions of the text of JUST DOGS: Harold Ober Associates, for "Dogs Are Almost Human" by Corey Ford, copyright 1953 by Henry Holt & Co., copyright renewed 1981 by John Stebbins and Hugh Grey; Irma O'Fallon Bales, for excerpts from "Duck Shooting," "My Dog Jim," "Hail and Farewell," and to reprint "Not Unsung" by Nash Buckingham; Charles Scribner's Sons, for excerpts from *Meditations On Hunting* by Jose' Ortega y Gasset; Charley Dickey, for an excerpt from "How to Help a Bird Dog"; Stackpole Books, for permission to reprint excerpts from *Drummer In The Woods* by Burton L. Spiller; George and Kay Evans, for various excerpts from *The Upland Shooting Life; A Dog, A Gun and Time Enough*, and *An Affair With Grouse*; Stone Wall Press, Inc., for "Missouri River Sandbar Geese"; Gene Hill, for "Lost Dog" and excerpts from *Tears & Laughter*; Bill Tarrant, for excerpts from *Hey Pup, Fetch It Up*, copyright 1979; Rosemary Thurber, for an excerpt from "Snapshot Of A Dog" in *The Middle-Aged Man on the Flying Trapeze*, Harper & Row, copyright 1935, James Thurber, copyright 1963, Helen Thurber and Rosemary Thurber; the Larry Sternig Literary Agency, for "All Ghosts Aren't White" by Mell Ellis; Charles F. Waterman, for an excerpt from *Gun Dogs & Bird Guns*; and Henry Holt and Company, for an excerpt from "My Dog Sam," and Liars Should Have Good Memories," and "The Reformation of Bo," from *The Best of Babcock* by Havilah Babcock, selected and edited by Hugh Grey, copyright 1974 by Alice Babcock and Holt, Rinehart and Winston, Inc. Reprinted by permission of Henry Holt and Company, Inc. Originally appeared in *Field & Stream*.

FOREWORD

In *Meditations on Hunting*, Jose Ortega y Gasset says that "Man has done no more than correct the dog's instinctive style of hunting, molding it to the convenience of a collaboration." Of course, and as any bird hunter will tell you, some hunters have, at one time or another, greater or lesser degrees of success in molding that collaboration, because every dog differs from the next, each is different, individual. Be it pointer or flusher, each dog the hunter shares his life with leaves with him discrete memories of individual style, of grace — or lack thereof — and of individual character. And each dog, too, is remembered singularly for the quality of its companionship.

But while bird dogs differ from one to the next, as do the characters of their wingshooting masters, they also share common qualities that bond them to the men with whom they hunt. The bonds of love and loyalty between hunting dogs and their masters, bonds strengthened by experiences shared in marshes and forests and fields, is what this book is all about. The hunter who sees his dog as only an animal, another tool of the hunt, like a shotgun or a pair of boots, won't appreciate what appears on the pages of JUST DOGS. But anyone whose Ben, Maggie, Parker, Thor, or Sally was ever at once his friend as well as his hunting partner, anyone who has ever looked into the eyes of his dog and seen there the soft, sweet look of fondness, of forgiving, infinite devotion, and felt that gaze all the way into his heart, will know what this book is all about.

Here, then, is JUST DOGS, a tribute to the wingshooter's hunting companion. Between these pages are photographic and written scenes from places and events familiar to anyone who has ever taken a dog and a shotgun afield. The literary excerpts, the short stories and photographs are designed to evoke memories of those dogs, living or dead, to whom the bird hunter owes so much.

The Editors

NOT UNSUNG

Nash Buckingham

Deep in every sportsman's heart is the love for some intelligent, intrepid animal. From the experience of fifty years of field and waterfowl gunning, I have worked and judged a great many top champions and competitors among bird dogs and retriever breeds. In the old days I have shot love-pigeon matches with such field trial champions as Powhatan and Ticonderoga retrieving for us. I have watched setters and pointers swim rivers and claw out of dangerously deep ravines, bird in mouth. I particularly recall my great old Chesapeakes, Baltimore and Pat o'Gaul. When I think of ensuing decades, I doff my hunter's headpiece to many another exhibition of dog initiative and accomplishment, such as the heroism of Henry Bartholomew's Fritz and Pat, whose exploits amid the Potomac's waves and razor-edged ice floes are still recalled around Broad and Swan Creeks.

On a rug near my desk lies a sturdy, ten-year-old English springer spaniel dear to me for his stout heart, faith in me, and an absorbing devotion to the gun. He minds my whistle and "hups" according to the rule book. But he also knows that it is strictly all right with me if he breaks shot when we are hunting in rough country. We lose too much game otherwise. That statement will bring "non-slip" purists about my ears but the perfect gun dog is the animal that understands its master's wishes.

Chub knows what I expect of him under any conditions. If a "sneak and crawl" is necessary, he is a master at it. Ordinarily, out dove shooting or where he figures we have a situation well in hand, he sits quietly beside me. But if we are on the move in high corn or flushing from matted cover, Chub breaks at gun-crack and is there if and when the game hits the ground.

The most memorable of Chub's retrieving performances came when he was a rough, hard-headed puppy of ten months. His initial yard and water work were well advanced; so I took him with me on a goose and duck shooting venture along a Mississippi River sand bar. This was encircled on the land side by a series of shallow ponds amid the willows and cottonwoods. We had a tiny shack hid out in that wilderness, fitted with comfortable bunks and a combination cooking and heating stove.

That morning a skim of ice glazed the long, narrow potholes. Chub and I sat down by one with a sliver of open water down its channel. A light breeze filtered through from left to right, and just after legal shooting hour a bunch of mallards swung past us downwind. Letting them pass unmolested, I sounded a low hail with my duck call and cautioned the quivering Chub. The big birds caught the summons, banked, and beat upwind, looking for what they had heard.

The pair I downed fell well across the hundred-foot water gut and on to dry land near tall, weatherbeaten willows. Chub was off, smashing through slush ice and fighting soft mud. Disappearing in the mutton cane, he emerged with his first find and battled his way back. After handing me the drake, he recast and soon presented me with our second prize.

For more than an hour that puppy worked boldly and untiringly. It would have been a superb job of retrieving for an older dog. During waits he sat beneath my sheep-lined coat, only to be off, eager-eyed, with the crack of my gun. When it was all over, I washed the blue mud from his coat and rubbed him dry. At the shack I cooked him up a bigger bait of ham and eggs than I consumed, with some sugared biscuits thrown in, and put him to snooze on my bed.

That afternoon we walked to the sand bar's end and sat down behind a rooty drift. We needed pre-supper exercise, and river sunsets are always glorious. Suddenly a gaggle of geese swung silently over the bar's rim, and I knocked one of them out of line. It tumbled fifty feet offshore and was swept downstream before I could walk halfway to it. It is easy, under such circumstances, to step off over some deep and hidden reef.

Past me swam little Chub. Outstripping the honker, he got a good hold and shoved his heavy burden ashore down the beach. Was I proud of him? Enough to stoop down and give the fellow a tight hug.

One of the most interesting afternoons I have ever spent behind a retriever was during November 1939, in a newly flooded pin-oak flat along Bayou Lagrue on the estate of Edgar M. Queeny, north of Stuttgart, Arkansas. Edgar, Dick Bishop, and I, with Grouse of Arden, Edgar's magnificent black Labrador, were exploring new territory for some high timber shooting. Our canoes raised hundreds of mallards as we slipped along the bayou, spilling over its banks in spots.

After finally going ashore, we waded through ankle-deep water to a long, narrow ridge that ended against a canebrake. Jess Wilson and Foy Dinsmore unlimbered their duck calls, and it soon became evident that great sport was prospect. Grouse had comparatively little to do until, after a particularly lively volley, three cripples sailed through the timber beyond the canebrake and disappeared. They must have hit water in the flat woods down the bayou. Dick and Edgar attempted to wade around the canebrake, but a deep slough threatened their boot tops.

I was using breast-high waders, however, and after some delicate stepping I made it across the "dreen" and into a far-flung fairyland of open water stretching away beneath low-hanging, sun-tinted foliage. Grouse swam across the deep chute, waited for me to land, and then, with a look that said "I'll be seeing you again," took off at a run through the backwater. Quartering against the breeze to catch the scent, the big black dog swung a half circle.

I sat down on a chunk to watch the proceedings. After a bit I heard a fluttering down the line of the canebrake, and here came Grouse with a winged greenhead in his jaws. Handing it over, he whirled and struck a left oblique across the woods. I could hear him splashing a long way off, but he was lost to sight. Then he fetched in a dead hen mallard. I had no direction to give him, and he didn't wait for orders. He was gone fully fifteen minutes that last cast, but returned with a badly crippled drake. Handing it to me gently, his eyes seemed to say, "That's gettin' 'em, ain't it?"

We rested a few moments while I gave him a taste of chocolate candy. Then we rejoined Edgar and Dick. It is well to inscribe such feats as that upon the pages of sporting lore.

There's another black Labrador I'll always remember. I was acting as an official gun at the Labrador Club of America's trials at Arden, New York in November 1939. Narrowed to a small field by the last day, the dogs and judges and guns faced a bitter low-ceilinged afternoon that drove alternate snow and rain across the mountain lake selected for final water work.

Roland Harriman, on whose estate the trials were held, and I shot from a huge, slanting rock some two hundred yards down the lake from the blind. As each two birds were dropped, some dogs swam to fetch, while others raced around the shoreline for a shortcut before hitting the water. It was getting late, and the fury of the elements increased.

We shot two ducks that fell farther out than usual. The Labrador whose turn it was ran around the land side, plunged in, swam swiftly to the first kill, and returned it to the blind. Then he returned and took up the quest for his second bird. Meanwhile the wind had blown his quarry in under the ledge of the rock beyond which Roland and I stood at the edge of the woods.

The Labrador swam around out in the darkening lake for several minutes, peering vainly for his duck. Then he swam to the rock and crawled ashore. Climbing to the rock's crest, he surveyed what lay beyond and spotted a keeper's boat tied in a lagoon behind us. Pricking up his ears, the dog trotted down to the boat, hopped in, and sniffed from bow to stern. In the stern, under a seat, he came upon a pair of dead mallards which the guide had retrieved and put there an hour or more ago.

Unseen, Roland and I watched the expression of bewilderment that came over the animal's face. Then he picked up one of the ducks and made his way over the rock's crest and down to the water's edge. Just as he was in the act of re-entering the lake, he came upon the duck that floated in against the ledge. He put down the bird he had found and taken from the keeper's boat and stood for an instant, lost in thought. Then, picking up the correct bird, he dashed across the rock, leaped over a fallen log to the shore, and raced to the blind.

The judges could not possibly have seen what transpired. But Roland Harriman and I watched the whole proceeding almost in awe. We could not, of course, mention what we had witnessed until after the awards were made. That dog was, as I recall it, placed third, possibly because he had been slow on his last find. Knowing what I knew, I certainly would have placed him first. That Labrador had a head and he used it.

There was something in that retrieve which was reminiscent of what I saw my greatest Chesapeake Bay retriever, Pat o'Gaul, do once in the high timber around our old Lakeside Club down in Arkansas. Pat and I stood at the edge of the woods along the open water. I took a long shot at a hen pintail that flashed past. I thought she flinched, but she kept on, circling far below us and curving back up lake over the timber. I noticed that Pat kept his keen yellow eyes on the duck for a longer time than usual; in fact, he wheeled around and stood staring after her for quite a while.

We shot there for an hour or more, then picked up and started to wade to our boat. But Pat, without so much as a "by-your-leave," bounced away inland and was lost to sight and sound. I waited at the boat and whistled and called a long time before he showed up. When he did, he had that same hen pintail, dead, in his mouth.

On Saskatchewan's wheat stubble and prairies, Edgar and 'Nuck and I discovered what our dogs, pointer Major and setter Billy, would do on chickens and Huns around the bluffs. Neither animal was experienced on such game, but thoroughly broken on quail. Billy, scion of the best in setter bloodlines, went wide and handsome, handling his birds intelligently and intensively. He caught scent a long way off and gave us opportunities at long rises that would have been longer otherwise. He worked the bluffs to windward first, circled them, and worked game cover entirely new to him as though he had been raised in it.

Major, on the other hand, never quite figured the thing out. If he scented in low cover, where he could sight the Huns or prairie chickens, Major flash-pointed, then crept forward until the birds flushed — and chased. But if he found them in high cover, Major proceeded just as the rule book said. After he had chased a chicken to the horizon, Major returned and offered his apologies.

We were shooting near Gainsborough, Saskatchewan. T. W. Jones of Corinth, Mississippi, who owns and operates his Canadian kennels for shooting and field trial dogs near Pierson, Manitoba, loaned 'Nuck and me a liver and tan ticked setter named Dan to replace a dog of ours who had sore feet. Dan turned out to be one of the most remarkable animals I have known. The first morning I had him out we worked the meadows along a winding creek, and the way he retrieved ducks from land or water made me open my eyes. But on Huns and prairie chickens the dog became a revelation. He was coming nine years of age, so his range had become somewhat shortened. But he was plenty wide for the country, and his stamina and courage were enormous.

With swinging lope, Dan ate up the open spaces, checkerboarding them with due craft of wind and nose. Striking scent, he whipped into fine, upstanding pointing postures, and, so help me, he had a way of looking around as we approached, as though he wanted to make sure that all was in readiness and our positions satisfactory.

Many times I walked in very close to watch his crafty stalk of birds that had run or fed off ahead of him. There was invariably the catlike stalk, a sort of shoving here and circling snakelike there, that eventually broke the rise from the most favorable vantage point to the guns. When the smoke cleared away, Dan, who had stood there like a hitching post, got down to the finest part of his act — retrieving.

From one bluff 'Nuck Brown and I raised a lot of game, Huns and chickens all mixed up together and flushing from every direction. 'Nuck fired at birds ahead of him, and I took care of flarebacks over the treetops. The ones we downed fell in the clear — out among the wheat stocks. We had seven on the ground, and Dan finally accounted for six of them. Then we moved to another bluff, and after giving it a going-over 'Nuck and I returned by the bluff where the seven birds had fallen. Dan, remembering perfectly, looked around a bit and brought in the seventh bird.

Another afternoon 'Nuck and I were tramping a well-bluffed wheat stubble. Suddenly, from over a rise ahead of me, sailed a prairie chicken, probably flushed some distance away by the incautious Major. Away it flew, under a full head of steam, and about four feet above the prairie. I swung in behind the bird, took six of its own lengths in forward allowance, and cut loose an ounce and a quarter of chilled sevens from my big duck gun. But nothing happened. A bit puzzled, I would have sworn I had landed some lethal pellets in that bird.

All at once that chicken's flight took a swift, and then swifter, upcurve. Higher and higher until, three hundred yards away, it crashed from fifty feet above the dead trees of a bluff. I even heard the crash as the heavy bird plummeted through the interlacing boughs.

About that time, Dan hove in sight, and I gave him the direction. I watched him deliberately get the wind on the bluff and start circling it. Then he disappeared. A few moments later he broke from that bluff with my bird, stone-dead and head shot, in his tender jaws. I had never moved from where I had fired.

Dan hadn't seen the chicken, hadn't seen me shoot. He simply took direction perfectly, used his fine brains and experience. He stood there for a few moments while I patted and stroked his grand old head.

We came, Dan and I, one bright forenoon, to a prairie meadow lush with bluegrass through which ran a typical wheatland creek — a mere rill in places, but broadening now and then into pools through which a lagging current rustled tall reeds. Here and there it was overgrown, or ran between high, weedy banks. Hunting parallel to this branch, I thought I saw a teal flutter above the stalks and relight. Without slowing Dan's range out along the edge of some wheat stocks, I walked quickly toward the creek. Thirty yards from it, through a break in the foliage, I saw that my supposed teal was a little blue heron. Another step, and the fellow took off with a croak. The next instant that waterway spouted ducks.

I bowled over two mallards and concentrated sufficiently to shove in a third shell and shoot at a lingering gadwall. All three ducks fell beyond the creek. Dan came on the gallop, took my directional wave at a glance, and swam the pool. Returning me a duck, he repeated the operation twice more, taking direction on each bird with almost human understanding. Never have I seen that retrieving job surpassed. Almost instantly, Dan sensed the fact that the upland quest had been turned into a duck hunt. Coming to heel, he worked the stream bends with an understanding equaling my own.

His crowning feat, however, came on our last day afield. Driving along that afternoon after a grand day's sport, we flushed a magnificent covey of Huns from the roadside. They settled around a clump of sparse buffalo willows in a deeply grassed pasture. 'Nuck and I left Bob Stoner and the dogs in the station wagon and tramped after the birds. They couldn't have risen better for the guns. Two to the left were downed, and another pair, escaping to the right, fell to my gun. I heard 'Nuck shoot twice, and he reported bowling over two with one shot. That made six Huns scattered over a space covering seventy- five yards of deep, dense cover.

We searched for fully five minutes without success. Bob Stoner, sensing our trouble, brought old Dan over on leash, and the fellow went to it. Starting at or near the point where my two birds fell, Dan crisscrossed the nearly waist-high grass with a probing nose. Down the line he went until five birds were sacked. But the sixth gave him a bit of trouble. Finally, he darted off into the meadow, whipped into a classic point and then dived headlong as a crippled Hun attempted to take off. Dan presented that bird to Bob with a look on his face which said as plainly as words, "What do you know about that guy's trying to put one over on the old boy?"

'Nuck and I said good-by to old Dan the last night we were in Saskatchewan. We dined that evening at the summer training camp of Mr. and Mrs. Chesley Harris, with T. W. Jones and his wife along to swell the festivities. Bob Stoner brought old Dan along from our last day's hunt to turn him back to T. W. There was one complex in Dan's make-up that needed explanation: he would positively not enter an automobile of his own volition. Once helped inside, however, he was perfectly happy and well behaved. T. W. said that, when a puppy, Dan had been hit and hurt by an automobile. The memory stuck, and he was as positive in that diagnosis as he was in his sensible way of handling and retrieving game.

The last time I saw Dan was after we fed him a feast of tender beef stew. Then Bob placed him gently in T. W.'s dog truck, and Dan, with a tired smile, sank into his hay bed. I wish him peace and rest for a life's work well done.

Out on the prairie, close to Chesley Harris' camp, is a tiny, beautifully planted graveyard. The chain-enclosed resting place is blanketed with petunias and roses. Up to it grows the wild plant life of those vast Canadian reaches. Beneath the flowers and pure marble grave covers sleep Becky Broom Hill, three times National Field Trial Champion, and McTyre, winner of not only the National title but championships on every species of American upland game.

'Nuck and Ches and I stood there in the chill, deepening twilight, looking down at their graves and thinking of the many times we had watched those champions in action, vibrant with life and courage and at the very peak of their magnificent careers. Turning away, Ches said, "I've told Mrs. Harris that if I die down home in old Alabama, why, bury me there; but if I happen to pass on while I'm up here on the prairies, to just put me here alongside these two. For that matter, I guess there's a part of me already there."

Maybe similar sentiment prompts my writing about Chub and Grouse and Billy and Major and Dan. Let's sit in our dens and clubs with our dogs and spin yarns about them and their deeds. For in every sportsman's heart there should be some gun dog whose deeds are not unsung.

All men who are dog men
walk a similar trail. The
butter-ball pup angling off to
one side, or the seasoned field
worker hired on for the gun,
or the gimpy, stoved-up senior
canine citizen who can't hear,
can't see, can't run — they
all walk to one side one time
or another in a dog man's life.

Bill Tarrant, Hey Pup, Fetch It Up!

. . . The best long range shotgun load to have in one's boat for mallards is a fine retriever.

Nash Buckingham,
Duck Shooting,
Field & Stream,
January, 1947

"The perfection of a life with
a gun dog, like the perfection of
an autumn, is disturbing because
you know, even as it begins, that
it must end. Time bestows the gift
and steals it in the process."

George Bird Evans,
An Affair With Grouse

Reason, which came to fill the gap left
by the evanescent instincts, fails in the task
of raising the suspicious game. For millennia
man gave this difficulty a magical solution,
and therefore, no solution at all. But one
day he had an ingenious inspiration, and in
order to discover the extremely cautious
animal he resorted to the detective instinct
of another animal; he asked for its help.
This is the point at which the dog was
introduced into hunting, the only effective
progress imaginable in the chase, consisting,
not in the direct exercise of reason, but
rather in man's accepting reason's
insufficiency and placing another animal
between his reason and the game.

Jose Ortega y Gasset,
Meditations on Hunting

Man has done no more
than correct the dog's instinctive
style of hunting, molding it to the
convenience of a collaboration.

Jose Ortega y Gasset,
Meditations on Hunting

Just because man
no longer understands
his place in the universe,
don't let him assume
all God's creatures have
become equally confused
and trivial.

Bill Tarrant,
Hey Pup, Fetch It Up!

Whoever said you
can't buy happiness
forgot little puppies.

Gene Hill

LIARS SHOULD HAVE GOOD MEMORIES

Havilah Babcock

The ability to lie is said to set man apart from the lower animals. When I say man I also include woman, because man embraces woman and because the weaker vessels have added certain refinements of their own. They have, so to speak, imparted to the art the polish of perfection.

Anthropologists do not know when man learned to lie, but certain it is that he has achieved a proficiency which leaves him unchallenged in the field. Man is admittedly the biggest liar because he is the most civilized of beings. It might be argued, indeed, that the invention of the lie marked a milestone in the progress of civilization.

But the bland assumption that the ability to fabricate a falsehood is an exclusive possession of *Homo sapiens* is altogether erroneous. The lower animals can lie too. In fact, their ability to lie often determines their ability to survive. Next to man, dogs are the biggest prevaricators. This is natural; they have been closely associated with man and have had many opportunities to learn. And the biggest liars are bird dogs.

I once owned a Llewellin setter named Belle who had an uncommonly cold nose. I have known her to pick up the trail of a peripatetic covey and unfalteringly follow their devious meanderings for a quarter of a mile until she found the right address and knocked on the door. When birds were scarce and she hit a cold trail, Belle would loll her tongue happily and say, "Now, you nice people just get comfortable and watch Miss Sherlock Holmes do her stuff."

But Belle abominated brier patches and would go to any length to avoid them. How many times have I watched her, head down and immersed in a trail, glance up to discover a brier patch just ahead. Abruptly she'd trail off at right angles and do her dramatic best to persuade me that, for some incomprehensible reason, the covey had at the last moment renounced sanctuary and ventured into an open field.

"Belle," I'd say, "you are an unmitigated fake and you know it. If you don't want your britches tanned, you'd better go into the brier patch and find those birds."

And she always did, looking like a small boy caught stealing licorice. "Okay, mister, you can't shoot a fellow for trying," she'd apologize. "When I'm hunting with your younger brother, I get by with it regular."

I once owned a big setter who abhorred cockleburs. Like Br'er Rabbit, he had no antipathy to a brier patch, but a cocklebur was anathema to him. Absorbed in a trail that led into a bur patch, Major would suddenly nose off in another direction with most commendable industry and convincingness. Indeed, it was his overacting that always excited my suspicion. Major never got by with his lying, but like some men he kept trying.

Another dog hated to retrieve a water-fallen bird. During wet seasons, especially in our southern low country, birds often fall into flooded savannas and bays. Whenever Chuck, who was normally a crack retriever, saw a bird hit water, he would begin to limp in a most distressing and heart-rending manner. The old malingerer, suddenly and unaccountably racked with pain, would miraculously return to health the instant another dog made the retrieve. The transparency and unprofitableness of his lying seemed never to discourage him. He had not pondered the wisdom of the adage, "Never tell a lie unless you can make it stick."

When I was a bird-hunting boy, my first dog sustained a broken leg under what might be termed compromising circumstances. Detected in the act of embezzling a turkey drumstick from the kitchen table, he departed via the nearest window, his exit being accelerated by a fusillade of brooms wielded by the irate womenfolk. Buck stood not on the order of his going but departed with such precipitancy that his parachute forgot to open.

For several weeks I showered attention on the invalid, with the result that when the leg mended he was, as my mother said, "spoiled rotten." Thereafter when he wanted something, or wanted to get out of something, he limped his way to success. But it didn't occur to me that he was feigning until the hunting season opened.

I soon observed that whenever I ordered him across the creek or into a brier patch he invariably began to limp, *but on the wrong foot.* The old malingerer had forgotten which leg he had broken, but it was too good a racket to abandon. The sight of me cutting a switch, however, possessed such remarkable curative powers that he promptly addressed himself to the business at hand. Two morals, I think, are deducible from the behavior of Buck: (1) a lie is a weapon that loses its edge if used too often, and (2) liars, like lovers, should have good memories.

"Speaking of prevaricating dogs," a friend of mine said, "let me tell you about one. A few seasons back I found myself overdogged and decided to sell one. A Yankee plantation owner hunted with me a day and was so pleased with Lone Jack that he bought him on the spot. But three days later the plantation owner brought him back. Lone Jack, he unhappily reported, had flushed every covey on 1,200 acres!

"Greatly puzzled, I hunted the dog the following day with another prospective buyer and found his performance flawless. So I sold him again, and again Lone Jack bounced back, the buyer swearing that in thirty years of hunting he had never witnessed such a graceless exhibition, and the proper destination for such a dog was obviously the nearest glue works.

"Again I hunted the dog, for several days this time, and found his performance beyond criticism. A week later I invited another buyer to hunt with me, but it proved a sad experience. Lone Jack made a shambles of the hunt. He flushed birds right and left, broke shot, chased rabbits, and wound up by devouring with great zest the only two birds we managed to get a shot at. The fellow left in disgust. Right then he wouldn't have swapped me a second-hand barlow knife for a sow and thirteen pigs. But after he left something occurred to me. Lone Jack had deliberately misbehaved to keep from being sold. The more I thought about it the more I admired him, and I quit trying to sell him. A dog who could lie as convincingly as that was too valuable to part with."

I once owned — but not for long — a barrel-chested pointer who imagined himself quite an actor. Old Muggs would find his part of the game and do a passable job of retrieving — beginning with the second bird. Somewhere in his devious past he had acquired a taste for raw quail, and he invariably gobbled down the first bird that was shot. During the rest of the hunt he abstemiously brought the birds in, apparently regarding the first as a sort of cover charge.

Having sneaked off and gorged himself, Muggs would gravely return and make a great show of looking for the bird he had just eaten. And, likely as not, with a telltale feather protruding from the old ham's mouth. In fact, he would almost catch an imaginary cripple as it scuttled into a brier patch or stump hole. I have known him to dig with the most admirable energy at the base of a stump for a bird his pancreatic juices had already half digested.

Old Muggs could have made himself a fortune in Hollywood. But I don't think he ever got there. What happened to him I don't know, but I rather suspect that he fell into the hands of some impetuous gent who didn't wait for that second bird.

A few years ago an elderly gentleman from Connecticut came down to hunt with me, bringing along a famously sired dog. He wanted me to see the scion of a national champion in action. Sunny Jim was a handsome ten-year-old pointer. Hunting with him and two active young setters of mine, we found birds aplenty. But an odd circumstance suggested itself to me during the first day: Sunny Jim was always with my dogs when birds were found. In fact, he was often ahead of my dogs on point, and to all appearances mine were merely backing him. But it still struck me as singular that Sunny Jim had not once pointed by himself.

The next day, while my guest from Connecticut was resting, I walked ahead and concealed myself near a pea patch where a bevy was sure to be banqueting. Presently my dogs came up and pointed. Sunny Jim, after looking circumspectly about him, warily inched forward until he stood in front. "The old embezzler!" I said. But I still didn't have enough evidence to hang him with.

It was not long in forthcoming. During the afternoon, while my elderly guest was napping in the car, I chanced to see a covey scuttle across the path ahead. Gloating over such a windfall, I called Sunny Jim — and watched him blunder into the skulking bevy without showing the slightest awareness of its presence. Just as I had conjectured, he had lost his sense of smell — as sometimes happens to aging hunters through illness — and he was bent on preventing his master from discovering his misfortune.

"Sunny Jim," I indicted, "you are a grand rascal and a consummate bluff. For two days you've been swindling my dogs and you know it. I'm going to expose you to you master right away."

But the old warrior looked so disconsolate and forlorn that I had a second thought. He was ten and his master was around 70, about the same age, I reflected. They were both nearing the end of their hunting days, and the chances were . . .

That night the old gentleman and his dog headed happily back to Connecticut with a dozen fat bobwhites neatly packed in his satchel. "What do you think of my dog?" he asked dotingly. "Didn't I tell you that — "

"You've got a remarkable dog, sir, a very remarkable dog," I answered. And it was a gospel truth.

The dog and I had both lied, but it wasn't the first lie I'd ever told, nor the last one. There are circumstances under which no gentleman will stoop to the truth. A lie is sometimes an act of charity.

On a famous plantation in low-country South Carolina there lives a gentleman who has become a legend during his own lifetime. At the age of 88 he is still an ardent bird hunter, as neat a quail shot as one could wish to see, and an altogether charming host with whom I occasionally hunt. While on his plantation a few years ago I heard a story I have been chuckling over ever since.

"Do you see that sad-eyed pirate over there?" an attendant asked, pointing to a rawboned pointer. "Well, he's the huntingest piece of machinery you ever saw, but he doesn't take any foolishness from another dog. Last year a Yankee brought a dog down here and allowed he'd show us how to hunt. The dog had three pages of ancestors, was just back from training school, and cut such a handsome figure that our boys called him Show Dog right off.

"We took Show Dog out with old Billy Bones there, and I'll be blest if that Yankee dog wasn't the pointingest thing you ever saw! During the first two hours he pointed two rabbits, five larks, at least fifteen stink sparrows, a Dominick rooster, and a bull calf lying in an okra patch. And every time old Billy Bones dutifully backed him.

"But just before dinner Show Dog broke his own record by marching up and making an All-American point on a sow and seven pigs lying in a pile of leaves. Billy Bones honored the point for a moment, then strode suspiciously forward to investigate. Discovering the object of Show Dog's infatuation, old Billy returned, leisurely lifted a leg and proceeded to irrigate the still-pointing dog, moving around from time to time to ensure good coverage. Then Billy Bones disgustedly headed for home. He knew when he had enough. So did the Yankee."

Dogs fool people, I suspect, more readily than they fool each other. A smart dog, having discovered that a hunting mate is an habitual liar, may refuse to honor his point or may show disapproval in some other way, but Billy Bones was admittedly unique in his method.

Unobserving hunters are sometimes too quick to fault their dogs, blaming them when they are blameless. That's why it takes a good hunter to keep a good dog good. To err is human; it is also canine. As a tight-lipped old hunter chided when I was a youngster: "Dogs just show you where the birds are. They don't hypnotize them."

More dogs are perhaps reprimanded for pointing stink sparrows than for any other cause, and more earn a reputation for lying on this account than any other. The stink sparrow is a tourist, raising in the North and migrating to the bobwhite country in the fall. It is a lowly groundling and hedgehopper. You are probably unaware of its presence until your dog suddenly stands transfixed in the broomsedge. You walk up expecting a thunderous rise, but nothing whatever happens, and you give your dog pluperfect hell for false-pointing — unless you chance to see a tiny sparrow take off unobtrusively, fly a few yards, and duck down again.

A knowing old dog may halt only momentarily, discover the error and resume hunting. Or he may wag his tail sheepishly and say, "Mister, I think it's just one of the little folks." But an inexperienced dog may make a federal case of it. For the stink sparrow is a puppy's partridge, a miniature bobwhite to catch the unwary. In the South puppies cut their teeth on stink sparrows, and don't let anybody tell you otherwise.

Certainly stinky is the most-pointed bird in the country, and few are the dogs that will not, for a disarming second, be seduced by him. During my long and misspent life I have never owned a dog that would not, under certain conditions, check his stride or waver for a second as a tribute to this fragrant groundling.

Field trial judges tell me that the stink sparrow is not unknown even in the best circles, and that solemn judges have been known to smile indulgently when some champion winked at the perfumed little coquette under his nose. But it's no use to blame the stink sparrow. He can't help stinking. And it's certainly no use to blame a dog, provided he quickly perceives his error and proceeds about his business.

When I was a country boy, I was a great bird hunter. The fact that I seldom hit anything deterred me not in the least. I still followed my elder brothers and hunted as hard as they did, but with this difference: whenever the dogs pointed, I always hoped it would be a stink sparrow so I wouldn't have to shoot and consequently wouldn't be embarrassed. When nothing got up, I was as good a shot as anybody else!

Bird dogs, whatever their capacity for prevarication, are far outstripped by the men who hunt with them. Bird hunters themselves have few peers as circumnavigators of the truth. As a matter of fact, few pastimes offer so many opportunities for lying as hunting. A good day in the field will give a fellow more opportunities to develop his talents than a week around the house.

For instance, your companion downs two birds on a rise and confidently hollers, "Dead bird! Dead bird!" to his dog. This is the most envied of all field commands and is uttered with a proud authority that echoes far and wide. You haven't clipped a feather, your shot either sailing off into the blue empyrean or hitting an unhappy sweet gum nearby. Never in your life have you felt less heroic.

Your loneliness is insupportable, your need for a face-saver never more desperate. So with all your imperfections on your head you, too, begin to holler, "Dead bird! Dead bird!" Then you go down on your knees with the dog and make quite a case of it — to keep the other fellow from suspecting the fraud. (Of course *you* have never stooped to such mendacity, not an upstanding, preacher-paying pillar of the community like you. *You* have never ordered a dog to find a nonexistent bird and bawled him out for not doing it.)

Perhaps most of the lying by bird hunters is done in an effort to extenuate their misses. Now, it is easy to miss a bird. It is easy to miss two birds, and a good hunter knows that no explanation is necessary. He gives none, he expects none. But the average hunter can invent more plausible alibis than a Philadelphia lawyer on court day.

I once took a professor of psychology hunting with me and got a brand new concept about this business of missing birds.

"Why did you miss that one?" I asked.

"Well, it was this way," he answered. "When the bird bounced up, my optic nerve transmitted the impulse from my retina to my thalamus. My thalamus transmitted it to the occipital lobe of my cerebral cortex. My cerebral cortex discussed the matter with my frontal lobe, which went into a huddle with my motor centers and spinal cord, which in turn communicated their findings to my muscles. By the time these outfits quit passing the buck, the damn bird was gone."

I missed the next five shots because I got to wondering whether my thalamus was doing the right thing by my cerebral cortex.

PLAY HOUSE

Oh! happy Boy; you have not lost your years,
You lived them through and through in those brief days
When you stood facing Death! They are not lost!
They rushed together as the waters rush
From many sources! You had All in One!
Why should we mourn
Your happiness? You burned clear flame, while he
Who treads the endless march of dusty years
Grows blind and choked with dust before he dies.
And dying, gives back to the primal dust
And has not lived so 'long' in those long years
As you in your few, vibrant, golden months,
When, like spendthrift, you gave all you were.

Anonymous

Their noses exquisitely
wise, their minds being
memories of smells.

John Masefield,
Reynard the Fox

Tell me, if you can,
of anything that's finer than
an evening in camp with a
rare old friend and a dog
after one's heart.

Nash Buckingham,
Hail and Farewell

THE LOST DOG

Gene Hill

Every time I stopped, the moonlight seemed to carry the slight tinkle of the dog bell I was listening for so intently. I stood there, heron-like, one foot in the air, afraid to put it down for fear that the slightest noise might mute the one sound I was waiting for. But the evening was a mocking one — I felt I might well have been searching for a leprechaun or stalking the pot of gold at the end of a rainbow.

I had last seen Pat at about 10 A.M. when she had found and pointed a woodcock. When I shot, she broke, as usual, since I wasn't too meticulous on that nicety, and up in front of us flushed a prime whitetail buck. Before this Pat had been at worst a five-minute deer chaser, just a little run to satisfy her instincts. I hadn't been overly concerned, but this time as they flashed through the woods I had the feeling that five minutes wouldn't get the job done. Twelve hours later, as worried as I was angry, proved my hunch.

As English setters go, Pat wasn't your "once-in-a-lifetime dog." She was stubborn, willful, and vain. But I had trained her to the point where, when all went well, I could get a decent day's shooting over her. But when all didn't go well it could be a disaster. Many days I simply gave up and led her back to the kennel in the station wagon, deciding to do the best I could by myself. I guess I kept her out for a variety of self-indulgent reasons: my refusal to admit I hadn't done as good a job of training as I should have; my tendency to spoil her and overlook the little hardheaded acts that usually led to bigger transgressions; and my plain softheartedness in refusing to come down harder and more often — a practice which might or might not have made a difference.

But by 10 P.M. all I could think of was a hurt dog lying in a roadside ditch waiting for me to find her, or a dog in the bottom of an abandoned well listening to my call and whistle and her answering bark tumbling back down on her in hollow, miserable mockery. I envisioned her collar hung on a wire fence, her foot in a forgotten fox trap. Anger and self-pity slowly gave way to fear and frustration so strong it nearly made me sick to my stomach. It was I who was the guilty one now and she the one needing desperately to have me with her.

I sat there listening to the night sounds. . . jet planes I'd rather have had been north winds. I'd rather the horns and screeching tires to have been the night calling of geese and herons. The sense of loss grew. Nothing comforted me. Everything seemed wrong. I felt like a small and simple man looking and listening for a lost dog while an impersonal, mechanical world went right on by without stopping to help or pausing to care.

The next day I told a friend I was upset about losing my dog, but he paid no attention to my grief; dogs are not worldly goods. That night I returned to where I had left my hunting coat with the slight belief that Pat would be there waiting for me. But the coat was an empty mockery of hope. I whistled and listened through yet another night, not knowing what else to do. Anxiety and fear were shoved aside by a feeling of futility and helplessness. The airplanes and traffic sounds made me feel more alone than ever before. I was on some strange sort of island.

I called the police but they showed little interest in only a lost dog. A check of neighboring houses and farms led to nothing. They promised to call if they saw a white English setter, but somehow I didn't feel encouraged. To them I was just an annoying stranger with a petty problem. I was a suspicious character to several, disbelieved by others, and, in my mind, ignored by all.

By now the night vigil had taken on another emotional aspect for I was searching for an unknown thing. Pat had become a symbol as real as any physical being. I needed to find her not only because I was committed to ending the mystery, but because I wanted to take her to these uncaring people and say, in effect, "Here is the dog I asked you about. See how much we enjoy each other; do you understand now how much it meant for me to have your help and understanding?" I wanted them to learn something about strangers and lost dogs and kindness, and caring enough to listen to the hurt of others with sympathy.

There was little sense in wandering around since Pat, no doubt, was doing the same thing, so I decided instead to find a spot to use as a post. I chose a long, slanting, fallen oak whose branches had caught in another tree. I climbed up, rested my back against a limb, and watched the evening mist beneath me like a silken sea. Here, suspended in space and time, my imagination was free to create a scene of a dog running a deer for a day, then, just as she is about to give up and come home another deer jumps in front of her, and then another. Unable to stop herself, Pat is led into a land she can never leave. I imagined a dog barking and another answering, then a third calling. My imagination flowed freely once again. One dog started barking and then dogs all across the country answered one another in an endless chain of howls in recognition of all that dogs have suffered at the hands of man in the cold light of the moon. I listened for a dog calling my name.

I placed a small ad in the local paper: LOST DOG, my name and telephone number, a description of Pat and the promise of a reward, but I had no faith in it. Almost a week had passed and I was running out of things to do; yet I felt I had to do something. The fading moon was just a twist of yellow like a discarded ring of lemon, making the night seem ominous. I brought a star book, laid back on my oak bed, and tried to memorize the Pleiades, Orion, and Betelgeuse. I thought of the ancient desert shepherds and their nighttime philosophies on the stars. I thought of their naked minds relating the unrelatable, glibly marrying suspicion, myth, and astrology, and trying to find a meaningful place for themselves while being surrounded by nothing except the incredible extension of their intellect. And I was bewildered when I thought how much of it had really worked out after all. But, in the long run, philosophy is a comfort only to philosophers and I am not really one of those incredible abstract thinkers — just a small, cold man lost in the woods, being hunted, I hoped, by a hungry, homesick bird dog.

I tried the old hunter's trick of imagining what I would do if I was a lost dog. Where would I go? What would be the limits of my endurance? But this was idle foolishness. Pat could literally be anywhere — around the next turn or in another world. The night vigil had lost its feeling of function and I took to driving around more and sitting less. A pointless use of time perhaps, by maybe, just maybe, I would find Pat.

I gave up when over a week had passed. I took the kennel out of the station wagon and avoided going near the dog run by the barn. My family had long since stopped talking about hunting in an effort to be kind to me, but it didn't matter. My own feelings were mixed: a sense of loss, a deep guilt, and worst of all, a nagging uncertainty. I didn't really believe Pat was gone. I couldn't conceive or cope with the idea of forever. I still drove around the area where she had run away, but more like a person trying to wake up from a bad dream than from any real hope of seeing her sitting by the side of the road, listening for the familiar sound of my car. People would recognize my car and wave, and a couple of kids knew me as the "lost dog man."

My mind searched for a simple solution. I imagined Pat had been hit by a passing car, then crawled into the woods and gone to sleep, undetected by the driver. It was neat, logical, likely — and unsatisfactory. Other possibilities came to mind but none were any better.

After two weeks the painful sense of loss faded, leaving a numb feeling of emptiness. I still caught myself listening for her bark when I pulled in the driveway, but the empty spots where she used to lie seemed ordinary again and I didn't think about feeding-time anymore. I felt better when I reminded myself that she was just an ordinary working field dog, nothing to brag about, spoiled, mischievous — and yet it hurt to remember that Pat was my dog in every sense of the word. She followed me everywhere, slept by my chair when I let her in the house and loved riding in the front seat of the car. The simple truth was that Pat had gotten to me in her own way, more than I had been readily willing to admit before. I felt almost ashamed to be so sentimental. It was difficult to imagine a man my age crying alone in his car for the sight of a small white dog. But it happened, and happened more than once.

This was all some time ago and I've never seen or heard of Pat again. I'm past grief now. Her image in my memory remains like a poorly focused snapshot of a white dog in an alder thicket — indistinct and distant like a ghost or a drifting wraith of mist.

They say that time heals all wounds, but that's not wholly true. Sometimes we can work around the reality and believe in a hereafter when we have to — imagining a lost dog living with someone else far away — a kind and gentle master who has discovered that she loves to ride in the front seat of the car with the window open, hates peanut butter sandwiches, and will, for no apparent reason, cock her head and stand stock still for the longest time as if she were listening for a faint whistling carried on the evening wind and the calling of a name she still remembers.

If you have done much chasing of bobwhite quail, you will recall days when you could not hit a flushing blanket with all four corners going in different directions. And when, after repeated misses, one of the old dogs turned from his lingering point and indignantly stared at you. Under such circumstances, I have seen a variety of eyes eloquently pleading for me to get on the stick or go home and sign up for skeet lessons.

Charley Dickey,
Florida Sportsman:
"How to Help a Bird Dog"
January, 1982

Every boy should
have a dog. It teaches
him to turn around
three times before
lying down.

Robert Benchley

HE'S JUST MY DOG

He is my other eyes that can see above the clouds;
my other ears that hear above the winds. He is the part
of me that can reach out into the sea.

He has told me a thousand times over that I am
his reason for being; by the way he rests against my leg;
by the way he thumps his tail at my smallest smile;
by the way he shows his hurt when I leave without
taking him. (I think it makes him sick with worry
when he is not along to care for me.)

When I am wrong, he is delighted to forgive.
When I am angry, he clowns to make me smile.
When I am happy, he is joy unbounded.

When I am a fool, he ignores it. When I succeed,
he brags.

Without him, I am only another man. With
him, I am all-powerful.

He is loyalty itself. He has taught me the meaning
of devotion.

With him, I know a secret comfort and a private
peace. He has brought me understanding where before
I was ignorant.

His head on my knee can heal my human hurts.
His presence by my side is protection against my
fears of dark and unknown things.

He has promised to wait for me . . . whenever
. . . wherever — in case I need him. And I expect I
will — as I always have.

He is just my dog.

Gene Hill, Tears & Laughter

BIRD DOG

Deep chest, slim flank, great heart to stand the pace,
And that unerring wizardry of scent
To trail the quarry in its secret place;
Power and cunning, speed and wisdom blent —
These are the immemorial gifts that came
Out of forgotten time's unfathomed gulf;
These are the fierce ancestral fires that flame
Undimmed, unchanging still — Son of the Wolf.

Grave eyes, grave bearing, dignity of kings;
The gentleness and trust as of a child;
The flawless poise that veils old savage things
But half-remembered from the vanished wild —
These are the knightly qualities that came
On unremembered fields where sports began;
This is the clear glow of a steady flame
Undimmed, unchanging still — Comrade of Man.

C. T. Davis

He had as much fun in the water
as any person I have known. You
didn't have to throw a stick in the
water to get him to go in. Of course,
he would bring back a stick to you
if you did throw one in. He would
even have brought back a piano if
you had thrown one in.

James Thurber, The Thurber Carnival

No day too long, no way too hard,
    nor toil, nor ice too thin,
For you to work your heart out,
    and always work, to win!
Sundown days! sundown days!
    Brave hunting there grown old,
But your champion's blood still urging;
    your noble heart still bold.

Nash Buckingham,
My Dog Jim

THE REFORMATION
OF BO

Havilah Babcock

"Is THAT the dog that hunted with us last year?" I asked. I almost put the question another way, but tactfully about-faced in the middle of it.

"You mean that ruined our hunt!" my host said with a wry grin. "Suppose *you* decide whether it's the same dog — after our hunt."

I cut an appraising eye at the big pointer standing apart with the guide and involuntarily winced as I recalled the incredible episodes of last year's hunt. Gladly would I have consigned the intractable young bandit — his name was Bo — to the bottomless pit, and in spite of the jauntily reassuring manner of my host I felt sharp disappointment.

Was this what I had driven to Georgia for? Had I known that I was to have Bo's dubious society again, I would have politely lied myself out of the whole business. But my host, Ben Carrington, was the most companionable of companions, and the shooting at White Hall, his spacious habitation, was perhaps unequalled in the state of Georgia. Besides, noting the intentness with which the dog studied the impassive face of the guide as if awaiting a cue, I privately conceded that there might be something different here.

When Ben Carrington had invited me the year before, Bo was not in the picture at all. Ben had dogs of his own, but within the space of a week four of them were incapacitated by one mischance or another, and Bo was hastily — and hopefully — acquired from a neighboring county as a last-minute replacement.

Be it said to the credit of Bo that his was not a negative personality. The handsome young dog swept the spacious flatlands with a boldness and verve befitting a scion of champions. Endowed with a remarkable nose, and that coveted indefinable known to the trade as bird sense, Bo was an efficient bird-finding machine. His pointing style, judged as an exercise in itself was unimpeachable, although I wouldn't have objected to a closer view of his work in this department.

The distance from which we were permitted to enjoy Bo's points was remarkably uniform: exactly five and a half steps short of shooting range. I have seen many flushing dogs in my time — perhaps I've been overblessed in this respect — but never one that had the thing down so pat. Time and again we hopefully slow-motioned the last few critical steps, but Bo's judgment of distance was uncanny. There was no outwitting him.

Nor have I ever seen a wrecker who put so much enthusiasm into his work. He'd hit a covey so hard that every bird instantly forgot family ties and took off on his own, devil take the hindmost. But covey wrecking was just the beginning.

Relentlessly Bo would pursue the stampeding birds and torpedo them one by one, barking each time in case we were keeping score. Having routed a covey to its last shreds, he would trot back to us with a self-satisfied air that seemed to say, "Well, gentlemen, that was a pretty thorough job, even if I do say so myself."

Ben was furious. "That damned fool has got the whole thing backward," he grimaced. "Thinks he's been hired to keep us from getting a shot. I'll guarantee it will take any land he hunts two weeks to recover!"

"Would you consider selling me half that dog?" I asked.

"Half? Why would anybody — " Ben was caught off-guard for a moment. Then he remembered *Pudd'nhead Wilson* and laughed. "So you can shoot your half, eh? Well, I'll be glad to take the offer under advisement."

Our only shooting was at birds stampeding over us, preferring, as Ben wryly commented, to face two guns rather than the four-legged cyclone up ahead. And we might as well have missed these. Whenever a bird fell, Bo would gallop up and bestir himself mightily in search of it. On finding it he'd trot off a mannerly distance, squat on his ample rump, and proceed to eat it.

Now a bird-eating dog is worse than an egg-sucking hound or a stump-sucking mule. Whatever the seven deadly sins of dogdom are, bird eating is the deadliest. But why dwell on it? I once had a history professor who, recoiling from an enumeration of the monstrosities of the Emperor Caligula, said in disgust, "The less said of Caligula the better!" Confronted by a "Discuss Caligula" question on a later quiz, I wrote one sentence, "The less said of Caligula the better," and made an A-minus on the course. It is that way about a bird-eating dog.

For a gallant game bird like the bobwhite to be pursued and digested by any other than a gentleman has always seemed to me morally inappropriate. But Bo, untroubled by ethics, proved himself quite a trenchman. During the afternoon he ate four birds, all we were able to shoot.

Now here I was, a year later, looking at the same dog, and what I was thinking was not for publication, because a dog who has acquired the Forbidden Taste is harder to cure than ten nights in a barroom. I hoped, therefore, that Ben would forgive me for putting a delicate question, "Has our friend Bo revised his gustatory habits?"

"Let us hope so!" my friend effused. Now, what kind of answer was that?

"And his tendency toward impetuosity in certain matters?" I politely probed.

"Let us also hope that our friend has learned to curb the natural ebullience of youth!" Ben wagged. He was talking like a politician being interviewed, careful to say nothing and to say it sonorously.

"If you've made a law-abiding citizen out of Bo my hat's off to you. How did you do it?"

"It wasn't me who did it!" he disclaimed. "It was him," he added, jerking a thumb toward the lanky guide leaning against the Jeep. "That fellow is something out of a book!"

"Looks the part," I said. "But how did he get into the picture?"

"After our disastrous hunt last year I decided to give Bo to the first person who would take him. That happened to be Aaron Church, who was doing some ditching for us at the time. Aaron used to boss a crew of mule-skinners at a logging operation in the swamp, and swampers still credit him with two talents — first, an unmatched capacity for forceful and picturesque expression, and second, the ability to decapitate a coiled rattler at twenty feet with a bullwhip. If you've never seen a real cracker, take a good look. By the way, know why they were first called crackers?"

"Can't say I do."

"Because of their skill at whip-cracking when they drove herds of livestock down the mountain trails. And do you know what made those whips crack?"

"I've never given these matters the benefit of my thinking."

"A whip cracks because it breaks the sound barrier. That's a little scientific jewel I came across the other day."

As we waited for lunch to be packed I studied Aaron Church with new interest. He was a man who would have gotten a second look in any company. Although he shuffled along with knees bent and neck forward like a turkey at a carnival, he was still a tall man. Through a rent in his hat a faded rooster comb stuck out belligerently. And his red neck blossomed with the bleached fuzz that my grandfather — trying to shame me into submitting to a haircut — used to call "po' folks" hair.

"Our lunch is ready," reported Ben. "Suppose we Jeep up and get started."

We were hunting the birdy flatwoods, an endless checkerboard of scattered pines and just-cut soybean fields that our southern quail have learned to relish. Here and there food strips of kobe and bicolor supplemented the beanfields, with always a background of the rippling broomsedge that is likely to frame any quailing picture in the Deep South. The spacious terrain gave a dog plenty of room to show his wares, and with the hawkeyed Aaron riding high in the pulpit behind us we were not likely to miss many tricks.

Within fifteen minutes his big fist hammered the Jeep top over our heads, and we stepped out to see Bo on point 150 yards away. With head high and tail arching over his back, he was a vivid tableau under the ancient and drowning pines. A gracefully pointing dog is to me a perennial delight — a scene which, however often beheld, has always a newness about it, one which never fails to bring me a quickening of the senses and a long moment's rapture.

But as we walked toward Bo I recalled another day, and anxiety dogged my steps. However, my concern was unwarranted. Not by the slightest movement did Bo hint his awareness of our presence, not even when Aaron, it seemed to me, unduly delayed breaking the spell.

"Take your time, gentlemen!" Aaron blandly invited. "We ain't hardly in no hurry a-tall."

And they weren't. After a while Bo covertly cut an eye at his lord and master, but it was only a polite inquiry and not a criticism. Nor did Bo budge from his unwavering stand until Aaron lifted a big hand and let it fall. That was the signal between them.

Now, it is considered impolite for a guest to outshoot his host, but having seen Ben Carrington handle his precious Parker 20, I knew I'd have to be lucky to be impolite. I was therefore untroubled by the amenities, and together we downed four birds. Bo went skimming over the ground until all four had been delivered to Aaron. Standing nearby, I noted the speed and tenderness of his bird handling.

One little byplay, especially intrigued me: when Bo brought in a bird, he'd stand by, prancing, until Aaron examined it. If there were no complaints he was straightaway about his business again. I grinned admiringly; here was quite a thing and apparently quite a dog. But how had such a transformation been brought about?

"Well, what do you think?" Ben beamed.

"Can't figure what method Aaron used to train him," I hinted hopefully. "A lot of other people would probably like to have his prescription."

"I'd hardly think they'd use it!" Ben laughed with great heartiness, as if something very funny, and very private, had occurred to him. "And I believe you'll agree when you hear about if after our hunt. Only Aaron — "

A big fist was hammering the Jeep top again, and we stepped out to see Bo waiting for somebody to take his picture. Throughout the mellow afternoon he continued to find birds, and I continued to marvel over the sureness with which he handled them. The finickiest judge would have faulted him not once. Any doubt I might have had as to the thoroughness of Bo's reformation was dispelled by two incidents, in themselves small but perhaps significant, which I observed during the hunt.

Hitting one covey quick and hard, Bo evidently decided he had cut the fuse a bit short. Ever so daintily he slow-motioned a backward step and replanted himself. Another time Aaron apparently had some question about a bird Bo had brought in. Squatting, he pointed out something and Bo became instantly concerned. Bo cocked his head and asked, *Would Aaron mind looking again? Couldn't that small skinned place have been caused by a shot or the bird's colliding with a wire fence?* But Aaron's probing fingers said he thought not, and Bo accepted the verdict. Maybe he *had* been a mite careless, he said, licking Aaron's hand, and he was glad to have his attention called to it.

During the hunt Bo found other occasions to report to Aaron. If a single he was pointing nervously jumped the gun, Bo immediately came in to tell his side and make sure everything was all right. What Aaron said, if anything, was inaudible to me, but it evidently exonerated Bo, for he raced joyously away.

Once during the afternoon, however, his standing with Aaron was open to question. But only for a brief moment, because Bo precipitately reconsidered. A shot bird had fallen into a canal and lay fluttering on the surface. The water was deep and cold, and Bo pretended not to see the bird. There was some awfully good hunting behind us, he said, trotting away and glancing back over his shoulder. Aaron leaned unconcernedly against a tree, saying nothing, and for a moment I thought Bo would win the argument.

But after a while Aaron quit fooling around, pulled a bird from his pocket, and carelessly dangled it in front of him. Instantly Bo dived onto the water, scrambled out with the bird, and went over to make a long explanation to Aaron. Why, I thought, should such an innocent gesture have such a remarkable effect on the dog? The question was still plaguing my thoughts when, as the shadows of the lordly pines began to lengthen, we counted our birds, shook hands heartily, and called it a day.

Then I went by to tell Ben Carrington's pretty wife how pretty she was, and to present her with a jar of quince jelly my mother had sent from Virginia. Mary was a Virginian by birth, and Virginians have a great predilection for quince jelly. Ben and I celebrated the hunt by a mutually agreeable swap: a quart of my golden scuppernong wine for a quart of his mountain peach brandy. And while we propped up the kitchen table and tested the comparative excellence of said potables my host recounted the story behind the reformation of Bo.

"I completely forgot about Bo after giving him to Aaron last year," Ben began, "and I wouldn't have thought about him again but for a remark Aaron made two weeks before the hunting season this year.

" 'Caught up with my work now,' he said. 'Think I'll break me a dog.'

" 'Have you got a dog?' I asked.

" 'Got myself Bo.'

" 'Oh!' I said, tactfully withholding further comment. 'Hope you luck.'

" 'Can't hardly break a bird dog 'thout birds.'

"Now, it was clear what Aaron was leading up to, but not quite.

" 'All right,' I said, 'you can shoot a bird or two across the swamp.'

" 'Season's not open,' he reminded me. 'Law'll cause trouble iffen you not with me.'

"I didn't exactly embrace the idea with enthusiasm, but Aaron was a useful man to have around. And I was curious to see the impact Bo and Aaron would have on each other. It would be like the irresistible force meeting an unmovable body that I used to hear about in the ninth grade, so I agreed and went along.

"I wasn't surprised to see Bo return to his bird bouncing with added zest, his appetite having been whetted by the summer layoff. But I was surprised to see Aaron put up with his lawlessness. Although Bo torpedoed a dozen coveys during the morning, Aaron remonstrated not once. Maybe he's sizing up the job, I thought — letting Bo build up a case against himself.

" 'Come tomorrer,' Aaron said after a while, 'we'll break us a dog.'

"Next morning he attached a long rope to Bo's collar and let him trail it around awhile. Let him knock up a few birds, in fact, so Bo would feel free and easy in his sinful habits. But when Bo began to make game near a patch of broomsedge, Aaron picked up the rope and strode forward, reaching Bo just as he bunched his muscles for the charge. Now, I thought, when Bo plunges forward Aaron will jerk him into the middle of next week.

"But Aaron was peering intently into the broomsedge, and, as if satisfied with his findings, he let the rope fall to the ground. Sensing his freedom, Bo hurtled forward, but he never really got under way. Aaron's big hands swooped down, carried Bo high above his head, and slammed him into the broomsedge.

"The thick broomsedge cushioned the fall somewhat, but Bo considered himself dead. Then he quickly decided that being dead wasn't the worst part of it, for he'd been dumped into a pile of birds skulking in the broomsedge. That was what Aaron had been looking for. As the amazed birds squirmed and wriggled in the broomsedge under Bo, went sizzling past his head, and even erupted from the vicinity of his privates, Bo decided

[76]

that judgement day had come and there were no hiding places left.

" 'Hear tell you lak to chase birds — that you jes' can't git enough of they society,' said Aaron, 'so I thought I'd give you a dose of your own medicine. Now tell me, did you git close enough to them birds to suit you? If not — ' Then Aaron propped his hands on his hips and engaged in further conversation with Bo. It was a little one-sided, maybe, but I must say Aaron acquitted himself well, even for a mule-skinning cracker.

"After a while Bo gradually reassembled himself, salvaged such dignity as he could, and managed to get going. Enough was enough, he said, sloping homeward. But a boy and a dog wake up new every morning, and when Aaron climbed into the Jeep the next day Bo jumped in behind.

"Again Aaron let him trail the rope, but no free flushes this time if you please! When Bo pointed, Aaron strode forward, keeping the rope tight as he went. But when he reached Bo's side, Aaron again let the rope drop, and Bo bunched his muscles for the inevitable charge. But to be on the safe side he cut an eye sideways and saw Aaron, great bony hands outstretched, hovering over him like an angel of death.

"Bo was nobody's fool and his ardor cooled down a bit. But neither was he one to give up easily, so there they stood for the longest — Aaron with arms upraised for an instant swoop, and Bo tremulously wavering between defiance and surrender. It was a contest of wills between man and dog, with the outcome uncertain for a moment. It sort of scared me to watch, but gradually Bo's body stiffened into a point, and Aaron's rough hand descended for a fumbling caress.

" 'Seen dogs I wouldn't hardly trade you for,' said Aaron.

"For the rest of the afternoon Aaron and Bo practiced together until they got the thing down pat, and Bo was handling his birds like a seasoned campaigner. Now and then Aaron would call Bo in and playfully rough him up, to the vast entertainment of Bo. Aaron shot on every rise, but he was careful not to hit anything.

" 'Reckon he'll think I'm helluva shot!' laughed Aaron. 'Got me a dog now.'

" 'What about his bird eating?' I reminded.

" 'One lesson at a time,' said Aaron. 'I'll start shootin' birds over him come tomorrer,'

" 'And when you do — ' I laughed.

" 'Break him from eatin' birds 'thout any trouble,' Aaron said casually.

" 'That will be the day!' I said.

"Now, as you know, there are as many recipes for curing a bird-eating dog as for removing warts by magic, and most of them are about as effective. I found myself wondering which of the usual methods Aaron would use, but it turned out that he used none of them.

"Next day Bo was stanch as a rock, and Aaron got a double on the first rise. He pocketed one while Bo picked up the other and, without breaking his stride, trotted off for a private repast. Aaron sat patiently on a stump and waited for Bo to finish picking his teeth. Then he said, 'A big boy like you oughter be able to eat more'n one,' and went back to hunting. Again Aaron got a double on the rise and Bo again collected half.

" 'Figger we need about one more bird apiece,' decided Aaron, and soon he had them.

'Now,' he said, calling Bo in, 'you got three, and I got three. But hit do seem to me that a stropping young fellow lak you could put away more'n that. Reckon you could manage three more?'

"And with that he flipped Bo over on his back, wedged him between his knees, and began pulling birds from his coat. 'Now you eat 'em and I'll count 'em,' he said. And he pried that dog's mouth open and — suppose we skip the gruesome details! I can't say exactly what happened anyway, because I turned my head away, but the sounds emanating from the broomsedge seemed to indicate that somebody wasn't having a very good time.

"When I turned back there were no birds left, and Bo had an amazed expression on his face and apparently an urgent need of privacy. As he trundled off he emitted a tremendous belch."

"Did Bo eat any more birds?" I asked.

"What do you think?" Ben laughed. "He became the tenderest retriever I ever saw. Mark Twain said a cat that has sat on a hot stove will never sit on a cold one thereafter. Guess that's the explanation."

"When Bo balked at going into the water, and Aaron held out that bird — "

"Blackmail," grinned Ben, "pure and simple. And you know what Aaron calls his remedy for flushing and eating? The overdose method."

"Well," I said, getting up to leave, "you have a great bargain in that dog."

"Don't know about the bargain part. Aaron charged me $500 for him. But when a man gets what he wants, I rekon he gets a bargain regardless of the price."

"Not one to argue with that!" I said, climbing into my car.

When I looked back, Ben was standing with his arm around his pretty, also very rich, wife. A bird hunter, being a practical fellow, seldom turns a pretty girl down because of her money.

It's not really important
that Tip was a good dog to
hunt over, but it is important
to me that she was a good dog
to be with. She was my pal.
We enjoyed being with each
other. I don't know that you
can ask for much more.

Gene Hill,
Tears & Laughter

A beautiful retriever
is like a virtuous woman.
Her price is far above
rubies. For retrieving is
what makes the difference
between a good dog and a
great one. It is the icing
on the cake, the cherry
atop the sundae, the lace
on a bride's pajamas.

Havilah Babcock,
Jaybirds Go To Hell On Friday

THE CURATE THINKS YOU HAVE NO SOUL

The curate thinks you have no soul;
 I know that he has none. But you,
Dear friend, whose solemn self-control,
 In our foursquare familiar pew,
Was pattern to my youth — whose bark
 Called me in summer dawns to rove —
Have you gone down into the dark
 Where none is welcome — none may love?
I will not think those good brown eyes
 Have spent their life of truth so soon;
But in some canine paradise
 Your wraith, I know, rebukes the moon,
And quarters every plain and hill,
 Seeking his master . . . As for me,
This prayer at least the gods fulfill:
 That when I pass the flood and see
Old Charon by the Stygian coast
 Take toll of all the shades who land,
Your little, faithful, barking ghost
 May leap to lick my phantom hand.

St. John Lucas

We never really own a
dog as much as he owns us.

Gene Hill, Brown Dog,
Tears & Laughter

The dog that will be worth watching, or shooting over, will be a virile, active, fiery-going dog that in puppyhood, or even in derby year, may be an impulsive, perhaps over-spirited, individual; but never a rattle-brained one. The difference between the over-zealous hunter and a crazy-headed one may be more difficult to discern in the beginning but by the time a dog gets into his second year the difference should be clearly discernible. Crazy-headedness is usually an ancestral trait, and if a young dog from level-headed mating shows signs of youthful wildness the chances are more than good that this is just the sign of a high class dog in a transitory period that, with the sobering process brought by age and judicious training, will develop into the very kind of a dog that goes to heights. Your grouse dog must develop grit, driving force,

and a special sort of reckless abandon to be rated as great, but he must also be tractable, easy to handle and direct, and ready to obey promptly and gracefully. This combination of almost dual characteristics is the big obstacle that confronts the man ambitious to own a high class grouse dog. It is also the reason why so many will describe their ideal as a docile, methodical, spiritless animal that never does wrong. These are the dogs of the men who fear spirit lest it get out of hand, and hot initiative lest it become uncontrollable. But they are not the men who have great grouse dogs, just so-so ones and these are not so hard to get, should one be interested.

W.H. Foster, New England Grouse Shooting

THE POWER OF THE DOG

Buy a pup and your money will buy
Love unflinching that cannot lie —
Perfect passion and worship fed
By a kick in the ribs or a pat on the head.
Nevertheless it is hardly fair
To risk your heart for a dog to tear.

When the fourteen years which Nature permits
Are closing in asthma, or tumor, or fits,
And the vet's unspoken prescription runs
To lethal chambers or loaded guns,
Then you will find — it's your own affair —
But . . . you've given your heart to a dog to tear.

We've sorrow enough in the natural way,
When it comes to burying Christian clay.
Our loves are not given, but only lent,
At compound interest of cent per cent.
Though it is not always the case, I believe,
That the longer we've kept 'em, the more do we grieve:
For, when debts are payable, right or wrong,
A short-time loan is as bad as a long —
So why in — Heaven (before we are there)
Should we give our hearts to a dog to tear?

Rudyard Kipling

ALL GHOSTS
AREN'T WHITE

Mel Ellis

Big water with its weird white fronts of fog does things to men's minds, and forgotten tales sometimes take on substance away out where the gulls fly patrol. Perhaps that is why men on the ore boats that ply the Great Lakes docked with stories of a big black Labrador, with a duck between its jaws, swimming through the mists many miles from any shore.

Sober men might have wondered what sort of ration the oreboat men were being served if it had not been that others also claimed to have seen the dog. Duck hunters fought snow storms back to shore to tell of a huge black dog, its muzzle white with frost. Commercial fishermen untangling nets said they'd seen the Labrador swimming through heavy seas, and they all claimed the dog had a duck between it jaws.

It was eight years since the first fisherman docked at Wisconsin's Fish Creek Harbor in Green Bay to ask if anyone had lost a Labrador as "big as a Shetland pony and black as midnight." I was stowing gear aboard a big boat for an island hunt and walked over in the twilight to listen.

"He stood on the point of Treasure Island and he had a duck in his mouth," the fisherman said. "We whistled but he couldn't hear me on account of the roaring surf. Then we edged in as close to shore as we dared without going aground, but he ducked into the brush. And yet there were no duck hunters out there today."

The next morning I combed Treasure Island with a friend whose name must even remain a secret, we'll call him Jerry. Treasure is the largest of the Strawberry group. We found huge imprints in the sand where a dog had run the night before. Thinking that maybe the animal had crossed to another island, we spent most of the afternoon searching three rocky outcroppings nearby. We killed a limit of goldeneyes while doing so, but found no further trace of the dog.

In Milwaukee that night I looked in the classified advertisements — and there was an ad promising a reward for the return of a black Labrador "lost on the Strawberry Islands."

Next morning I phoned the man who had advertised and told him what I knew. For obvious reasons, I'm not going to reveal his name, but will identify him only as R.J.H.

"That's Jeff, all right," he declared. "I wouldn't give a penny reward for him if I didn't know a guy who'll buy him as soon as I can get a rope around his neck."

As I hung up the receiver I hoped R.J.H. wouldn't get his dog back. I didn't know exactly why I felt that way, but somehow he chilled me.

Next day I called Jerry. I started off by telling him about this R.J.H. who had lost his dog. "You haven't seen the Labrador, have you?"

"What did you say the man's name was?" Jerry asked.

I repeated the name. "Know him?"

There was a long silence. Finally Jerry said that he did, that he had guided for the man once, but that he'd never let him set foot on one of his boats again. I wanted to go into it further, but long-distance telephone calls cost money, so I figured to take it up with Jerry the next time I saw him. After I'd hung up I remembered that Jerry had forgotten to say whether or not he'd seen the dog.

On a hunch, I phoned the editor of a field-trial publication. He knew the man and told me about him. Said that while judging a field trial he had disqualified the fellow for abusing his entry.

That afternoon I shot some pigeons for a retriever trainer named Chuck, who lived north of Milwaukee. He knew the man, too — had trained the dog for him. "And what a dog!" he said. "One of the most promising youngsters I've ever seen."

"What about the man?" I asked.

Chuck frowned and talked reluctantly. But between his story and the editor's I could piece the picture together. Evidently here was a dog completely loyal to a man who gave him nothing but abuse.

Chuck told me he'd asked the man to leave his place after he'd kicked the dog for failure to remain steady on the line. "But the dog stuck to him," Chuck said. "I've seldom seen retrievers take that sort of treatment and keep coming back for more. But that was the kind of dog Jeff was. Once he set out to do a thing, he stuck to it until it was done — whether it was making a retrieve, whipping another dog, or licking this guy's boots. You figure it."

I couldn't, so I forgot about it until about a week later, when the man who had lost the Lab called again. He wanted to know if I'd heard anything further. I told him I hadn't and — intrigued by now — asked him how he'd lost the dog.

"The fool went out after a goldeneye and just didn't come back," he said.

"Just didn't come back?" I repeated incredulously.

"That's what I said," R.J.H. replied. "The duck was a cripple and he followed it. I whistled, but he kept going."

"But," I said, "you went after him in a boat, didn't you?"

"Not on your life I didn't. It was blowing. I wasn't going to get wet. Water was coming over the gunwales and it was freezing."

"Oh," I said, and hung up.

I had the picture now, and it wasn't a pretty one. The man had been hunting a small island north of Treasure Island. The dog had never heard the whistle above the pounding surf. Intent on completing the retrieve, Jeff had become lost out among the big waves and eventually wound up on the wrong island.

I felt sure someone would pick up the dog, but three weeks later it was apparent that no

one had, because the man called me again. "I think somebody is keeping my dog," he said.

"Maybe you're right," I agreed. "But how are you going to prove it?"

"Oh, I can prove it if I can locate the dog. I've got my initials R.J.H. tattooed in his left ear."

Winter came in quick that year. I didn't hear from R.J.H. again, but the following spring and summer I heard rumors of a big black Labrador being sighted in the vicinity of the Strawberry Islands. It wasn't until fall, however, that an Associated Press story came across my desk quoting a commercial fisherman as saying he'd seen a Labrador as huge as a small horse on the shores of Treasure Island — a dog carrying a duck.

It was a good story as such stories go, but I threw it in the wastebasket. For one thing, I didn't want R.J.H. to read it. Not that I believed the fisherman, but some people might. And a good newspaper doesn't encourage the circulation of stories having no basis in fact.

Less than a week later one of our correspondents sent in another story telling how three duck hunters had seen the big black dog silhouetted against an early-morning moon on the rocky point of the island, staring out toward the open water. He was still carrying the duck.

This time I couldn't ignore the story. State papers were picking it up. Nobody believed it, but to them the apparition was symbolic of the perfect retriever roaming endlessly through a world of water and sky with no thought but to complete his retrieve.

That winter R.J.H. kicked one dog too many and was brought to court for cruelty to animals. This was the first time I'd got a look at him, and I didn't like what I saw. That made it still more difficult to understand how a dog could give so much love and loyalty to a man who deserved it so little.

I finally filed big Jeff's love for R.J.H. in the same pigeonhole in which would be filed the love story of a woman who follows a no-good husband straight through hell to be by his side. It was one of those things you don't figure out — just accept.

I wrote and told Jerry what had happened to R.J.H. A night or so later he phoned me and spent nearly $10.00 in toll charges telling me how he figured R.J.H. had got just what he deserved. That wasn't like Jerry, so I wondered after he'd hung up why he was so concerned over the fate of a man he guided but once.

For six years, then, the stories kept coming in. Sometimes bass fishermen would see the dog on a summer evening as they fished the reefs that ring the islands. The year the lake trout started to make a comeback, anglers bobbing through the ice told of a black dog trotting across the frozen horizon carrying a duck in its mouth.

It made intriguing copy unless you knew about R.J.H. and then it was kind of sickening. A score of times I was tempted to write the true story of how he'd deserted the dog. I figured the animal had starved the first winter, no dog could survive on those bleak islands. But when you're a newspaper man you never forget the law of libel, so how could I write about a scoundrel who'd abandon his dog to the elements? How could I write about a dog that had given his heart to a man who didn't deserve it?

I even searched for the animal's bones one spring while up bass fishing. But the islands have many bones of gulls and of crippled ducks that crawled ashore to die, of animals washed ashore, and even of Indians. I found no clue.

Several times I dropped off to see Jerry, but he was always out fishing. Then one fall there were no more stories about black ghost dogs, so I checked with Associated Press and they put a query on the wires. I called our correspondent on the lake front, and he talked with a score of duck hunters and commercial fishermen. But no one had seen the dog for nearly six months.

I supposed the story had just sort of worn itself out, that men had wearied of hearing it, and that those who visited the Strawberries didn't see the dog now because their imaginations had no news-story stimulation. In a way I was happy about it. It was one story I was content to let remain half written. I hadn't seen R.J.H. in years, and that was all right too.

I hadn't seen my friend Jerry either, and I was happy to get his call to come up to the islands for a hunt. "The goldeneyes are down this year, like they've never come through before," he said.

He knew that would get me. Shooting goldeneyes when they come whistling down from the Arctic with icicles goosing them all the way is a sport comparable to none. You hunt the big water and you fight ice on the decks, and waves coming over the gunwales, and snow in you eyes.

Jerry's dogs greeted me. There must have been six or eight in the kennel in back of the house, and they roared a welcome when I drove in. It was good seeing Jerry again after all those years. After dinner we sat in the living room, and it was then I noticed the big Labrador on the rug beside the chair.

"Going in for house dogs?" I asked.

Jerry laughed self-consciously. His wife had never let him bring a dog into the house. "This one is retired," he explained. "I retired him about six months ago."

Six months ago? I couldn't help remembering that it was just about six months ago that the last of the "Black Ghost" stories had come across my desk. I wondered. Jerry had retired lots of dogs in his time, but that hadn't meant they could come into the house to wait their lives out. I knew there was more.

"Good dog?" I asked.

"The best," Jerry said.

"Had him long?"

"Quite a while."

"Buy him from someone around here?"

Jerry nodded. "In a way you might say I did. Bought him, that is."

I leaned over then and flipped the Lab's left ear so that the initials R.J.H. were visible.

Jerry shifted uneasily in his chair. "To be honest with you — " he began.

"You don't have to honest with me," I interrupted. "Just tell me, when did you find him and did he still have the duck?"

Jerry walked over, knelt, and took the dog's graying muzzle between his hands. "I had him the very first night you called. I was about to tell you — I intended to tell you — but

[98]

then you mentioned the name of the guy who'd lost him. I knew then I'd never tell anyone."

The Lab's tail beat a soft sound against the rug.

"Did he have the duck?" I asked.

"He had a duck. I don't know if it was the one he was chasing the day he got lost, or a cripple he'd picked up. You know how hard it is to kill goldeneyes. You know how the crips are always coming ashore in a blow. It might have been a crip."

"But — " Questions crowded to my mind. "How about the villagers, the hunters, the fishermen?"

Jerry scratched the dog's muzzle gently. "I knew they'd be looking for him. But I'd see Jeff dead before I'd let that louse get him back. So I locked him in my island fishing shack. He broke out a couple of times. Some of the oreboat deckhands and hunters must have seen him. Maybe he was even picking up cripples. I suppose that's how the stories got started. Then, just before the big freeze, I brought him home."

The big dog sighed. I sighed too, and as a man turns the page of a long, long book, I turned the big Lab's ear down to hide forever the initials R.J.H.

"Until you have bred dogs and have drawn and painted them, it is difficult to realize that no two are identical in conformation. You need do no more than gun for a day over two of them to recognize that each is an individual. It requires the intimacy of daily living with a dog to know the subtle quality of his mind, the ham-smell of his ears, and that his wet nose in your mouth tastes salty."

George Bird Evans,
A Dog, A Gun and Time Enough

I like them all —
pointers, setters, retrievers,
spaniels — what have you.
I've had good ones and
bad of several kinds.
Most of the bad ones
were my fault and most
of the good ones would
have been good under
any circumstances.

Gene Hill

Puppy days! Oh! puppy days!
Potlicker, rabbits and fun,
From dewey dawn to locust's song,
nothing to do but run!

Nash Buckingham,
My Dog Jim

I think we are drawn to dogs
because they are the uninhibited
creatures we might be if we weren't
certain we knew better. They fight
for honor at the first challenge,
make love with no moral restraint,
and they do not for all their
marvelous instincts appear to
know about death. But being such
wonderfully uncomplicated beings,
they need us to do their worrying.

George Bird Evans,
Troubles With Bird Dogs

MISSOURI RIVER SANDBAR GEESE

Charles L. Cadieux

Like any close relation between two people, there will be an occasional clash of intents if not of wills, and you must work this out without loss of intimacy

George Bird Evans, *Troubles with Bird Dogs*

When the spring thaw broke up the ice, the Missouri became a raging torrent, carving the river banks anew with huge chunks of ice — rearranging the geography so that we had a different river to hunt over every year. Sometimes those spring torrents brought down a motley collection of decoys, which had been left on sandbars the fall before.

Some of these were tire decoys. An arc was cut out of the body of the tire, becoming the body of the goose. A head and neck were sawed out of a one-inch pine, and the whole works was painted flat white or flat gray to simulate blues and snows. From checking hunters, I knew they worked. I got a chance to hunt over them with Jake Gottlieb.

Jake stood six foot six in his waders, and weighed in at 290 — 40 pounds of which was fat. We floated over to a sandbar in his aluminum john boat, carrying guns and ammo, forty tire deeks, lunch and coffee and a double armful of dried cottonwood branches to make a rude blind. Butch, a bucket-headed Chesapeake retriever, scorned the boat and swam alongside across 100 yards of swirling water to reach the bar.

We set the decoys facing into the northwest, which was also upriver. Cottonwood sticks with the leaves still hanging on were poked into the sand to form a blind. "Just enough to break our silhouettes," Jake instructed. It would have taken quite a few branches to mask his huge form, even when he was lying flat.

With everything arranged, Jake waded to the other bank and tethered the john boat. Then he waded back. "Even if they do spot the boat, it'll help us," he said. "They'll shy away from it and move closer."

Our first customers were a flight of green-winged teal, which Jake disdained. "Not enough meat with the cost of shells what it is today!"

Next came a duo of mallard hens. "Take them if you want to," Jake offered. I was slow getting up and dropped only one of the hens — out there a "fur piece" in the swirling current of deep water.

Butch stood up, almost yawning, and looked at Jake. "Fetch," and Butch trotted down to the downstream end of our bar, plunged into the fast current and swam strongly to intercept the duck. Snapping it up, he reversed and vectored across the current back to the bank about 150 yards downstream. Without stopping to shake, he trotted up the bank to the quiet water and walked across to the blind. He dropped the duck, then shook heartily, spraying me thoroughly.

"Good dog you got there," I offered.

Jake looked pleased, but he said, "The bastard is too hard headed to suit me."

About 9 o'clock Butch was staring to the south and we heard the distant honking of whitefronts. Eleven geese were beating their way upriver against the light wind. Jake said, "I believe I can talk to those specklebellies." He did, giving as good an imitation of the "toodle-doodle" high-pitched quaver of the whitefront as I'd ever heard. The birds went on past, swung to the call and came in upwind, looking for a landing spot.

"Wait till they're over the bar," Jake whispered. I knew what he meant. It would be rough for the dog to retrieve geese dropped out in the current.

We jumped up and started shooting. I dropped two — one in the shallow water to the west of the bar, the other on the dry ground at the south end of the bar. Jake dropped two in the shallow water.

Butch raced into the water and started retrieving. He brought both of Jake's birds, dropping them alongside the hen mallard. Without hesitating, he headed out for the bird I had dropped in the water. As he picked it up and started in, Jake was grinning broadly. "I'd rather eat speckles than all the Canadas in the world," he said. "This calls for coffee. Whaddaya say?"

He was pouring coffee into the red plastic cups when Butch dropped the third bird with the others. He was blowing on the hot coffee when he saw that Butch was returning to his waiting position.

"What's the matter with you, you dumb bastard?" he yelled at the dog. "Can't you see that goose in plain sight there on the sandbar?"

Butch turned to look at the goose, but flopped down on the sand, one watchful eye on his oversized master.

"Oh — ho!" Jake bellowed. "So we're gonna be like that, eh?"

"Probably can't see it," I suggested, although the goose was in plain sight less than fifty yards away.

"The stubborn bastard sees it all right," Jake snorted. He walked over and stood beside the dog, which rose to all fours, warily watching Jake. Giving the dog a line with his forward- swinging arm, Jake commanded, "Fetch!"

Looking back a quarter of a century later, I can still hardly believe what happened. With a savagery totally unanticipated, Butch leaped for Jake's throat! Only the big parka saved Jake from that initial leap. Now, I've seen dogs being playful and sometimes playing rough. I've seen dogs bluffing, and they can be realistic. Butch was neither playing nor bluffing. He was trying his damnedest to kill!

Knocking the dog away with a mighty sweep of his arm, Jake faced the second attack. Butch roared back, again leaping for the throat. He was met with a right uppercut from Jake's mitten-clad, ham-sized fist. The punch knocked the dog sideways. Before he could scramble to his feet, Jake dove on him. Swatting ferociously with his big mitts, Jake batted the dog's head, somehow avoiding the savage snap of those big jaws.

Grabbing a thick fold of hide on the scruff of Butch's neck, Jake slammed the dog repeatedly against the sand. Then he knelt on him. Whaling away with his free hand, Jake wore himself out on the dog, which finally stopped trying to get loose and lay still, absorbing fearful punishment.

Arm weary, Jake struggled to his feet, still holding onto the thick fold at the back of Butch's neck. Jerking the dog into the sitting position, Jake roared, "Sit!" Butch sat!

Jerking the dog ninety degrees to the right, Jake pointed him toward the dead goose. "Now, you sonofabitch," he yelled, "fetch!"

Butch took off at the dead run, scooped up the whitefront on the gallop, returned it stylishly to the pile, then went back to his position and flopped down to watch the swirling river.

I had stood there motionless, my shotgun at the ready, all through the battle. I guess I had in mind to defend myself, if need be. "My God, Jake! What got into Butch?"

Jake waited till he quit puffing, took a sip of his coffee and looked at Butch with a tolerant grin. " 'Bout once a year, me and him go to the mat," he said. "Got to show him who's boss, then he's okay for another year or so."

"I wouldn't keep a murderous bastard like that ten minutes." I said. But Jake answered, "Geese!" and dove for his blind. I got hidden in time to see a small bunch of blues and snows riding the wind downriver, making knots. They made a half-hearted turn toward our spread, so I put out my imitation of a lonesome snow goose. They circled, but the circle didn't get any smaller. "We better take 'em," Jake exclaimed. "They ain't coming closer!"

We fired a total of four shots. One loner slanted down, wing-tipped, but trying mightily to stay up with the flock. He lost altitude in a long, flailing glide across the current, slammed into the undercut clay bank and fell into the river. Once in the water, he righted himself and began to swim up against the current.

"Fetch." Butch showed his intelligence by running 100 yards upriver before plunging in. True to his proud Chesapeake Bay heritage, he swam with great strength, but the mighty Missouri was pushing him southward with greater force. He kept his eye on the goose, changing directions when it did. When the goose became aware of the dog, it turned to swim downstream.

Swept up with the fast current, dog and goose went out of sight around the next bend, and Jake splashed over for the john boat.

"He'll never get that one," I said.

"Let's see if we can give him a hand," Jake said. "That water is fast and cold — cold even for a Chesapeake!" We fired up the little outboard motor and sped down with the current, searching the water far ahead. We had gone more than a mile when I caught a movement of white out of the corner of my eye. There was Butch, walking north along the bank carrying a very much alive snow goose!

Heading back upriver, Jake yelled over the noise of the motor, "What was you saying about not keeping a dog like Butch around?"

. . . making no noise either with foote or with tounge,
whiles they followe the game. These attend diligently vpon theyr
Master and frame their conditions to such beckes,
motions, and gestures as it shall please him to exhibite . . .
(In making mencion of fowles my meaning is of the
Partridge and the Quaile) when he hath founde the byrde,
he . . . stayeth his steppes and wil proceede no further,
and with a close, couert, watching eye, layeth his belly
to the grounde and so creepeth forward like a worme . . .
neere to the place where the birde is, he layes him
downe, and with a marke of his pawes, betrayeth
the place of the byrdes last abode.

Caius, Royal Physician to Elizabeth I

There are some dogs,
like some people, who won't
listen to reason and who
respond only to a lick
on the tail.

Robert Ruark,
Old Dogs and Old
Men Smell Bad

It was like just meeting you
made his day. He quivered with
excitement. Rolled over in
submission. Nuzzled up so's
the warmth of his body came
soothing to your heart
through the skin of your
ankle. So you picked him up.
That's the way with love.
It's contagious.

Bill Tarrant,
Hey Pup, Fetch It Up!

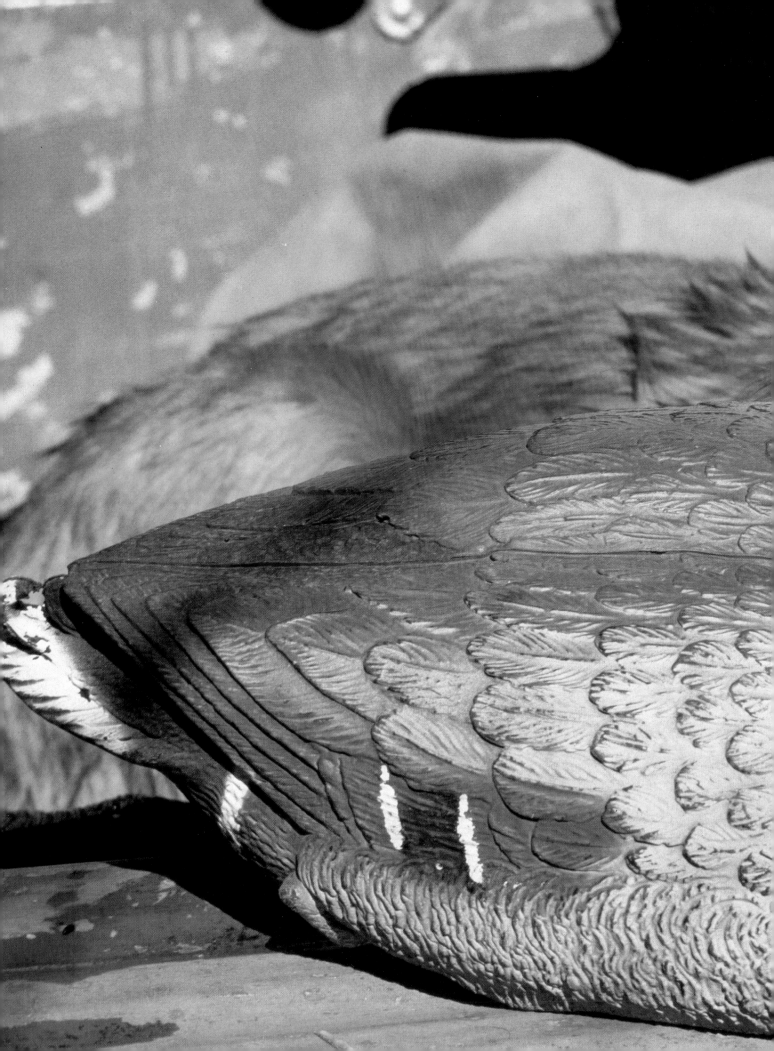

She used to obey
a look and a nod, but
now she acts like a
willful old spinster.

Guy Valdene,
Making Game

TO A DOG

So, back again?
                — And is your errand done,
Unfailing one?
How quick the gray world, at your morning look,
Turns wonder book!
Come in — O guard and guest;
Come, O you breathless, from a lifelong quest!
Search my heart; and if a comfort be,
Ah, comfort me.
You eloquent one, you best
Of all diviners, so to trace
The weather gleams upon a face;
With wordless, querying paw,
Adventuring the law!
You shaggy Loveliness,
What call was it? — What dream beyond a guess,
Lured you, gray ages back,
From that lone bivouac
Of the wild pack? —
Was it your need or ours? The calling trail
Of Faith that should not fail?
Of hope dim understood? —
That you should follow our poor humanhood,
Only because you would!
To search and circle — follow and outstrip,
Men and their fellowship;
and keep your heart no less,
Your to-and-fro of hope and wistfulness,
Through all world-weathers and against all odds!

Can you forgive us, now? —
Your fallen gods?

Josephine Preston Peabody

DOGS ARE ALMOST HUMAN

Corey Ford

The monthly meeting of the Lower Forty Shooting, Angling and Inside Straight Club was over a little sooner than usual, owing to a slight altercation between Judge Parker and Doc Hall over their respective bird dogs. As Colonel Cobb said later, you can argue with a man about religion or politics or even women, but you can't argue with him about his dog.

The whole thing started when Judge Parker's pointer growled at Doc Hall's setter. They didn't exactly fight, but they walked sort of stiff-legged around each other and the hair stood up on the backs of their necks, and the Judge said "Shut up, Timmy" and Doc said "Toby, I'm ashamed of you, quarreling like that." They pulled the two dogs apart. "I never saw Timberdoodle act that way before," Judge Parker apologized to the Club, "but I guess he isn't used to seeing another dog racing around, upsetting things and ruining the furniture."

"I don't know what you mean by that," Doc Hall bristled, "just because October likes to get up in a chair. He sleeps in the same room with me, and he's very well behaved."

"Personally I don't believe in spoiling a dog," Judge Parker said, "not if you want to make a good hunting dog out of him."

"Then what's your dog doing right now," Doc demanded, "lying on the sofa?"

"He's lying on top of my hunting coat," the Judge said, "waiting for me to take him out. Pointers are very intelligent."

"Toby wouldn't lie around and wait," Doc Hall said, "he'd pick up the coat and bring it over to me. That's the difference between pointers and setters."

"I suppose you're going to tell me that a setter has more brains," the Judge said indignantly.

"Of course he has," Doc retorted, his voice rising. "A pointer is just a machine. A setter *thinks*."

"Reminds me of a very intelligent bird dog I had once," Colonel Cobb interrupted, filling the glasses from Uncle Perk's jug. "I was leading him down the main street of Boston, and he came to a solid point on a total stranger. I knew my dog never made a mistake, so I asked the stranger if he was carrying a bird in his pocket, and the stranger said he wasn't. So I asked him if by any chance he'd been handling a grouse lately, because I never knew my dog to be wrong before, but he said no, he never saw a grouse and he wasn't even a hunter. So I had to apologize for my dog, and I shook hands and said 'I'm sorry, sir, my name is Cobb.' 'Pleased to meet you,' the stranger said. 'My name's Partridge.' "

Judge Parker and Doc Hall emptied their glasses in unison. "But to get back to what we were saying," the Judge resumed, "a setter just tags at your feet. I'll take a pointer if I want a day's hunt."

"Most of the day," Doc said, "you hunt for the dog."

The Judge glowered. "At least, a pointer's steady. He'll bang into a point and hold it all afternoon."

"A setter knows better than that," Doc Hall said triumphantly. "Toby'll back off a point and come get me, and lead me back to where the bird is. A setter's more dependable—"

"A pointer don't bump birds—"

"Like that dog of mine I was telling you about," Colonel Cobb broke in quickly, filling their glasses again, "I was hunting him late one fall, and he disappeared and I couldn't find him. I looked all night, and all the next day, and then it came on to snow and I had to give up. Well, sir, next spring after the snow melted I happened to be walking through that same cover, and there was the skeleton of my dog, still solid on his point, and right in front of him was the skeleton of the grouse he'd been holding." He sighed. "That's what I call staunch."

Judge Parker and Doc Hall gave him a cold glance. "As I was about to point out," Doc said, glaring at the Judge, "a setter will figure out the cover, and the direction of the wind, and he'll find more birds in an hour than a pointer could find in a week, because he's got sense. He's almost human."

Judge Parker swallowed his drink in a gulp. "I s'pose you think your dog's more human 'n' my dog," he shouted indignantly. "Why you take Timmy—"

"I wouldn't take Timmy," Doc taunted, "if he was a gif'."

" 'F you'd like to step ou'side," said the Judge, rising unsteadily and peeling off his coat, "I'll show you which dog is more human or not."

"Okay 'th me," said Doc belligerently, taking off his glasses, "we'll settle this thing righ' now."

"Wait a minute," Colonel Cobb said, pulling them apart. "Why don't you settle it right? We'll take both dogs out to the White Church tomorrow, and turn 'em loose, and see which one finds the most birds. The winner gets a jug of Old Stump Blower."

"I'd like to enter that contest, too," said Dexter Smeed. "I got a little dog out in the car, name of Fluffy."

"Who ever heard of a bird dog named Fluffy?" said the Judge sullenly.

"I got it from some friends that found it," Dexter said, "it's not exactly a setter or a pointer either, it's got a short tail and one ear flops down and its coat looks like a moldy piece of bread, but it can hunt because it got into a skunk the other night, so I thought I'd bring it along and see what it could do."

"I tell you what, Dexter," the Colonel said, "you better leave Fluffy in the car tomorrow. The other two dogs might get discouraged."

The Club got an early start the next morning, and all the members went along on the hunt except Dexter, who decided he'd better stay in his own car and keep Fluffy company. Doc's setter and the Judge's pointer each got a bird on the first cast, and then they moved on into the big alder cover beside the brook and disappeared. "Toby's solid on a point somewhere," Doc said, "if we could find him."

They hunted a couple of hours, and Doc started blowing his whistle, and the Judge shouted himself hoarse, and they both fired their guns, but there was no sign of the dogs. The only sound was the steady honking of Dexter's horn. At last they turned back and headed for the road. Dexter's car was parked by the church, and the pointer and the setter were jumping up and down beside it and whining and panting to get inside.

"Call your dogs off," Dexter shouted, rolling down the window a crack, "before they scratch all my paint."

The Judge and Doc didn't even look at each other. They broke their guns, and ran to the dogs, and grabbed them by their collars. "I never saw Timmy quit a hunt before," Judge Parker admitted sheepishly.

"I wish I knew," Doc muttered, what got into Toby."

"Maybe I should have mentioned," Dexter said, "that Fluffy's in season."

There was a moment's silence. Colonel Cobb picked up the jug of Old Stump Blower and presented it to Dexter Smeed. He gazed at the two dogs thoughtfully.

"It only goes to show," he murmured, "that dogs are almost human."

MY SETTER, SCOUT

You are a tried and loyal friend;
              The end
   Of life will find you leal, unweary
Of tested bonds that naught can rend,
   And e'en though years be sad and dreary
Our plighted friendship will extend.

A truer friend man never had;
             'Tis sad
   That 'mongst all earthly friends the fewest
Unfaithful ones should be clad
   In canine lowliness; yet truest
They, be their treatment good or bad.

Within your eyes methinks I find
             A kind
   And thoughtful look of speechless feeling
That mem'ry's loosened cords unbind,
   And let the dreamy past come stealing
Through your dumb, reflective mind.

Scout, my trusty friend, can it be
             You see
   Again, in retrospective dreaming,
The run, the woodland and the lea,
   With past autumnal streaming
O'er every frost-dyed field and tree?

Or do you see now once again
                    The glen
          And fern, the highland and the thistle,
And do you still remember when
          We heard the bright-eyed woodcock whistle
Down by the rippling shrub-edged fern?

I see you turn a listening ear
                    To hear
          The quail upon the flower-pied heather;
But, doggie, wait till uplands sere
          And then the autumn's waning weather
Will bring the sport we hold so dear.

Then we will hunt the loamy swale
                    And trail
          The snipe, their cunning wiles o'ercoming,
And oft will flush the bevied quail,
          And hear the partridge slowly drumming
Dull echoes in the leaf-strewn dale.

When wooded hills with crimson light
                    Are bright
          We'll stroll where trees and vines are growing,
And see birds warp their southern flight
          At sundown, when the Day King's throwing
Sly kisses to the Queen of Night.

When shadows fall in life's fair dell,
                    And knell
          Of death comes with the autumn's ev'n
To separate us, who can tell
          But that, within the realm of heaven,
We both together there will dwell?

Here is the dog, which has always been an enthusiastic hunter on his own initiative. Thanks to that, man integrates the dog's hunting into his own and so raises hunting to its most complex and perfect form.

Jose Ortega y Gasset,
Meditations on Hunting

A dog anticipates pleasure and fear but I like to think, and I believe I'm right, that he does not anticipate death, though he may sense it when it happens to another and he has carried death in his mouth with each retrieve. At any period of your life the most aging thing you can do is to think in terms of being old. You should, instead, emulate your old gun dog who as a puppy spent his energy burning up the country but now paces himself, going directly to birdy places, handling the birds with finesse gained by years. And when the old fellow lies beside you by the fire, his dreams are of what he has done that day and is eager to do tomorrow — not about when it is going to end. That lesson from him in his Indian Summer is not the least of what he will have taught you in your long, good life together.

George Bird Evans,
Troubles With Bird Dogs

SO LONG, PAL
Burton Spiller

When I first met you the shooting season had ended, and the leaden New England skies seemed doubly cheerless because I had just lost your predecessor. Into that somber period of my life you came like a sun-kissed morning. I recall the day perfectly.

I was sitting morosely by the fire, pondering why a malicious fate so often casts a somber shadow over our lives. Then your owner drove into the yard with you and five of your brothers and sisters. I remember that when we opened the crates and you all came tumbling out pandemonium immediately ensued. Such leapings and twistings and turnings! Such mad dashings across the field! Such a turmoil of yelpings which filled the air with their clamor, and dwarfed to nothing the exuberant cries of skaters rioting on the river, yet strangely it was a soothing sound to me. The leaden skies seemed to lighten, and all at once there was warmth and friendliness in the crisp December air.

I wish I might tell you that I knew from the first moment that you were going to be my dog, but that would not be strictly true. There were too many of your kind, a liver-and-white kaleidoscope that would not be still a moment. But gradually I became aware that there was one bit of atomic energy that frequently separated itself from its fellows and returned to its master for a friendly word. That was you, old boy. I knew you then. You were a one-man dog, and you were going to be mine.

I have never regretted my decision, and I like to think that in all the years we were together you never had occasion to regret it either. You see, I had formed an opinion concerning the ideal relationship between a dog and its master which was somewhat at variance with my youthful conception of the status. I had learned that a dog was as much an individual as was a man, and I had come to believe that as long as it was compatible with good bird work, a dog should be encouraged to express his individuality. If he had his own ideas concerning the best way to handle a running pheasant or ruffed grouse, it might be better for me to modify my views slightly, instead of trying to mold the dog to my inflexible will.

I had vowed, too, that by every artifice at my command I would try to make my dog think that I was the most wonderful person in the world. He should be taught to mind promptly both signal and spoken commands, but there would be no hint of harshness in the teaching. Firmness, yes, but a gentle firmness that would leave no taint of unpleasantness for him to ponder over when he was alone.

And so I opened my home to you. You had your tufted pad in the kitchen. You owned one end of the davenport in the living room, and the upholstered chair in the den was yours by divine right. From the other rooms, and from the chambers, you were barred, but after you had worked your way into the heart of the gracious lady of the manor, I could sometimes hear the stealthy pad of your feet upon the stairs as you inched your way upward and into her room to wriggle an ecstatic good-morning welcome.

I remember how your soft brown eyes finally won for you, and how after a time you would remain there until you heard me open a door which led outside, when you would come tearing down, leaving a devastation of scattered rugs behind you, and vault in a long, arching curve out into your great and beautiful world.

Then you changed from a gangling six-months pup, whose feet and one end or the other were always a size too large, into a sleek and muscular creature whose every lithe movement was so graceful that it would cause a constriction in my throat just to watch you. We were compatible, you and I, for my system worked in your training. Five minutes time was all that was needed to teach you to hold as steady as a rock on your plate of food, and you won your sheepskin in retrieving after six easy lessons.

From the first day I took you afield you hunted with a joyous lightness that was my conception of perfection. Your nose spurned the earth as did your feet. You were airborne from the moment we entered a cover until we emerged from it, flitting here and there before me as smoothly as a swallow, while with your head uplifted you quested the air for game scent, yet slowing abruptly and advancing with tiptoeing caution whenever your unerring nose caught the first elusive fragment of it.

How wonderful they were, those first magic days that we spent together in the woods. The surrounding hills were no more immovable than you when you stretched out in one of your glorious points. No command of mine could move you as long as a ruffed grouse crouched in a thicket before you, as you proved to me on one of the very first days we hunted together.

You had disappeared from my sight in fairly thick cover, and after waiting a decent interval I drifted ahead with hope that I would find you on point, but you were not there. With hurrying strides I went the length of the cover, and emerged into a more open one where only a few scattered pines grew. You were young and ambitious, and I thought the open country had challenged you to explore it; so I covered that, too, fearful lest I had lost you, and wondering if you had picked up enough woods lore to enable you to pick up my trail and follow it.

I was blowing my whistle then, shrilly and at frequent intervals and, still blowing it, I returned to that part of the cover where I had last seen you. There was one small opening in that tangle of birch and alders and by mere chance I blundered into one end of it. There you were at the other end, locked in a fiery point that a half hour of waiting had not quenched by a single degree.

There was always something about your points which made me a better man with a gun. You were so infallibly right when you slid into that animated but immobile pose, that it sometimes lifted me to supreme heights. So it was on that occasion. The grouse rose at a thirty-yard range and had less than ten more to go to reach screening cover, yet I killed it without any sensation of hurrying and I had several feet to spare.

In the woods you were a dog who could be depended upon to the last minute of the day, but at home you were sometimes unpredictable. I recall the occasion of Ray Holland's first visit with us. No one had told you that Ray was editor-in-chief of *Field & Stream*, and that he was paying for much of your bread and butter, or you might have acted differently.

Everything was normal for a time, and then that awkward moment arrived when conversation suddenly lagged. I was groping desperately for a topic, like a circus elephant wondering where the next peanut is coming from, when I thought of you.

You had a queer little trick of curling your right forefoot inward and lowering your head a trifle, and I had elaborated upon it until at a secret signal from me you would make a deep and exquisitely polite bow. We had rehearsed it until we had it perfected, and now it seemed like a life-saver. I went out and got you, put you smartly at heel, and we came in snappily like the well-trained pair we were.

In the doorway I paused abruptly, said, "Pal, this is Ray Holland," and took one step aside, which was the cue to do your stuff. In that sudden and awful silence, you looked at him calmly up and down, from his slightly thinning hair to the tips of his well-polished shoes — and yawned prodigiously. Then, with an air of melancholy that only Hamlet could have equalled, you turned and went back to the obscurity from which I had summoned you, and curled up on your mat to resume your interrupted slumber.

There was another occasion when we entertained equally distinguished guests at dinner. Everything was painfully formal and polite, and so far as real genial warmth was concerned we might as well have been dining in an igloo. Then my ears detected a sound which filled me with startled apprehension. It was the sound of your teeth clamping down on the metal rim of your food pan. You came bounding in, your nails screeched as they brought you to a skidding halt beside the table, you banged the dish down on the floor, took a backward step and looked expectantly up at us as though to say, "Hey, you guys! Don't I rate a plate of food from a setup like this?"

You got the food, as you undoubtedly knew you would, and it was the Most Distinguished Guest who passed the collection plate, but even before you had finished bolting the last fragment a miracle had taken place. All our stiff formality had vanished, and we were really enjoying a friendship which has been a lasting one.

I remember, too, the day when you gave me the coldest bath I have ever experienced. We were hunting woodcock in the Nighthawk Cover, a mile-long strip of alder tangle through which ran a brawling, turbulent brook. It was late in the season. The ground had frozen the previous night, and even now with the sun two hours high there was a rim of ice around the edges of each upthrust boulder in the brook.

We had hunted the length of the cover, and now I was searching for a place where I could cross the stream. Ordinarily there were numerous spots where one could step from stone to stone and win the opposite bank with feet still dry; but on this day the water was far above its normal level and the stepping-stones were few and mighty far between.

I found a place which showed possibilities. It was not entirely to my liking, for it required five jumps, and the third one — in the center of the stream — was at least three feet out of line. The trick would have to be accomplished at high speed if it were accomplished at all, and I had a growing conviction that to pivot on that rounded boulder in midstream, and then spring off at a tangent for the remaining two, would require perfect co-ordination of both mind and muscle.

Standing on the bank, and deliberating the problem of which foot should touch which stone, I became so engrossed that I forgot another and equally important factor. The most rigid schooling I had given you consisted of crossing a street in the midst of heavy traffic. I would put you at heel and wait for a favorable opportunity. When it presented itself, I would tug mightily on your leash and we would shoot across the street in nothing flat. You learned to do it perfectly after a time, adjusting your pace to mine so accurately that we were never separated by more than a few inches. That was the factor I should have remembered.

Clutching the gun in one hand and my hat in the other, I leaped for the first boulder, and from the tail of my eye I saw your agile form take flight at the same moment. The situation, I could readily see, was about to become complicated unless I was man enough to beat you to the other shore. No boulder had room for more than one foot at any time, and to attempt to place five on it simultaneously could only result in disaster.

I beat you to the first one by inches, but we struck the second one together. Somehow I managed to secure enough leverage to make that twisting, third leap, and I made it with a sure foreknowledge of what was about to happen. It was necessary for me to achieve quite a bit of altitude in order to span the distance, but your wiry muscles gave you a flatter trajectory. You were fairly on the boulder and contracting your sinews for another leap when I came down upon you. You emitted one startled yelp, which was dwarfed to insignificance by my resounding splash, and then the icy waters closed over us.

You were the first ashore, and with a vigorous shake you were ready to go again, but I had to strip off the last dripping thread and wring the water from it. Ah, me! We were thirty miles from home, and we were hunting woodcock. We took our limit that day, with a brace of grouse thrown in for good measure, and we went home after night had fallen, dry and warm and inordinately happy.

One of the most satisfying things about the years we hunted together was the fact that I never knew you to fail to find a crippled bird. I believe a dog requires a far keener nose to locate dead or crippled game than he does to find an uninjured one, but whether or not this is true you had the thing required. You surprised me many times by bringing in a bird I believed I had missed cleanly.

There was a day when we were hunting woodcock along the shores of Lake Winnipesaukee. It was exceptionally open cover, and there was absolutely no excuse for missing any bird that got up within range; but I did it on a perfect straightaway. It was so entirely unexpected that I was disconcerted for a moment, and instead of redeeming myself with the second barrel I watched the bird fly a hundred yards and then flutter down into another sparse clump of alders.

You always gave me a puzzled look whenever I missed a bird, and on that occasion I could plainly read the question in your eyes. "What's the matter, boss?" they asked. "Slipping?"

I admitted it and told you to go find that woodcock. "Show him to me once more and I'll prove to you whether I'm slipping or not," I said, and you went down the cover and locked up on another of your spectacular points.

I kicked the bird out, killed it cleanly and sent you in to get it. Somehow you were never really enthusiastic about bringing in a woodcock. Knock down a grouse for you, and you would rush in and grab it, then come bounding back with a million-dollar light in your eyes, but the little russet fellows always left you emotionally cold. Your attitude seemed to say, "It's swell sport hunting them, boss. I like to point them and I like to see you bowl them over, but what the heck do you care for them after they're dead?"

So you went dutifully in after the bird and started out with it. Then you hesitated, slowed to a walk, stopped, dropped the bird and began working the cover at your right.

I said to you, "Haven't you heard that a bird in the hand is worth two in the bush? Cut the fooling around, get down to business and bring me that bird."

You might have been deaf for all the attention you gave me. Methodically you quartered the thicket, swung sharply left, picked up a woodcock and came plodding out with it.

"I killed the first bird after all," I thought, but carefully refrained from voicing more than a polite thank you when you dropped it in my hand, for I was curious to learn if your reasoning powers were equal to the occasion.

If there was even a suspicion of doubt in my mind, I'm sorry for it, for of your own accord you went back and found the bird you had dropped, then came bounding back, passed it up to me, and your look seemed to say, "How's that, huh? Don't you think I'm a pretty good sort of a guy to have around?"

I always thought your were. I miss you. Only yesterday I found myself pausing with my hand on the open door as I waited for the familiar thud of your feet as you landed beside me. You had an habitual disregard for those first three steps, and always went from the bottom to the top in one effortless leap. Undoubtedly I shall wait thus for you many more times. I wish it were possible for you to know that.

You left an impressive volume of memories for me to cherish, but of them all I think the last time we hunted together will remain clear the longest. For weeks I had known the disquieting feeling that you would not be with me much longer, but when the veterinarian told me so it came as a distinct shock. There had always been the hope that a miracle might happen, but now I could no longer hope. Yours was a tremendous vitality, for you rallied at times until you seemed almost your old self, but always when the relapse came you sank a little deeper into the abyss that awaited you.

Then the shooting season opened. I am very positive that you were aware of it, for your knowledge of many, many things was always a source of wonder to me. Your eyes followed my movements more closely during the hunting season, and once again I was keenly aware of them, even when you were apparently dozing before the fire.

Then one morning, after the frost had rimmed the lowlands with its white lace, you came to me with one of my hunting shoes in your mouth, and when I took it from you you went and found its mate. "Want to go, do you?" I asked, and with all the animation your spent body could summon you answered "Yes."

I am glad that I decided as I did. My life has been richer because of those few last hours we spent together in the woods. There was a cover by the river, a scant three miles from home, that always held a few woodcock. By jouncing the car for a mile over corduroy roads I could put you within a half mile of it, and I knew your gallant heart could carry you the rest of the way. This day was yours. Nothing could take it from you.

You got down from the car like an old, old dog, but there was a crispness in the fall air, a heady odor to the moldering leaves which seemed to breathe new life into your emaciated frame. Your head came up, your questing nostrils searched the stirring air, and your lance-like tail assumed its old-time merriness.

You found a woodcock at the very edge of the cover, a second and third in a little depression near its center, and the fourth and last as we circled back to the outer edge. The legal limit was four, and we gathered them in with only four shells. Better than we had done on some other occasions you could recall, eh, old pal? But it was fitting that it should end thus, for they were the last woodcock your glorious nose would ever locate. When you came out with that last bird your hunting days were over. Finished. Done.

And you were done, too, old man. The fire which the day had kindled in you flickered and died as we started back, and your legs gave way beneath you. I gathered you up in my arms, an almost lifeless load, and started back toward the car.

We had almost reached it when all at once I felt you stiffen in my arms. For a moment a quick dread seized me, and then I knew. Your head was uplifted. Your heavy eyes had opened wide and assumed a new brightness. Your extended nostrils were expanded and drank the crisp air in quick, excited inhalations. Ruffed grouse! Somewhere in the thicket just ahead that mottled brown king of the uplands crouched, poised on taut sinews for its hurtling ascent. Ruffed grouse! Generations of your ancestors had lived and died in order that there might be inculcated in you an inherited instinct which made the scent of ruffed grouse the acme of all your physical senses. It was the excuse for your being. Without it you never could have lived.

I lowered you gently to your feet, a spent creature who had shot his bolt and who was well-nigh done to death by an hour's toil. You swayed in your weakness, but the magic of hot grouse scent was in your nostrils and it was still potent. The trembling left your legs, your head lifted and you took four cautious steps ahead. A pause, another infinitely cautious step and you had it, straight and true from the fountain head. You froze into immobility. A pitiful caricature of the thing of fire and bronze you once were, but invincible still. You had nailed your grouse.

I pushed the gun forward and stepped up behind you, and in that moment we became omnipotent. We were gods who ruled that little kingdom of birch and alder and scented fir. You in your infallibility had located the quarry, and I was possessed with the sure knowledge that no tumultuous ascent, no artifice of twisting or dodging which was his heritage could suffice it in this moment of its dire need. This thing had been foreordained. It was something which had to be.

The grouse came out on thundering wings, scattering the brown leaves beneath it with the wind from its takeoff. Upward it careened, a flashing, brown projectile, and your eyes watched the startled flight.

The nitro crashed, and the bird hung limply in the air for a moment, suspended by its own inertia, before it hurtled down to set up a spasmodic drumming with its spent wings upon the fallen leaves.

"Dead bird," I said, and you went in and brought it out to me, and I could see a bit of heaven shining in your eyes.

I like, too, to remember the few last minutes we were together. You lay on your bed, covered by your blanket. The lethal dose of sleeping potion was already beginning to circulate in your veins. Your eyes were heavy, but in them there was a contentment and peace.

Then a little pointer pup, a liver-and-white replica of what you must have been before I saw you, came up and sniffed a friendly greeting to you. Your eyes opened a trifle wider, and beneath your blanket your hard tail beat a friendly response. You extended your nose, sniffed your approval of the little stranger and bade him welcome. You knew there must always be other dogs, and so your great heart accepted him and shared him with the one you loved. It was all that was left for you to give. Then you yawned sleepily and closed your tired eyes.

So long, Pal.